WHAT THE LOCUSTS
HAVE EATEN

A ROADMAP OF RESTORATION AND RELATIONSHIP

J. M. Ulmer

ISBN 978-1-0980-6143-2 (paperback)
ISBN 978-1-0980-6144-9 (digital)

Christian Faith Publishing, Inc.
832 Park Avenue
Meadville, PA 16335
www.christianfaithpublishing.com

Printed in the United States of America

I would like to thank the following people for their direct or indirect part in making this book possible:

My wife Karen for her love, support and her heart for Christ, Colleen Brown for the cover idea, Tiffany Morrow for her work in the early stages on editing, Bev Browning for great insight in writing, Patrick and Linda Callahan for their encouragement, Daina Skinner for encouragement and a great haircut. I would like to thank all of those that prayed for me along the way.

CONTENTS

INTRODUCTION

First, I would like to say that I am not a writer by profession. I have a regular day job, and I volunteer at a local church. Beginning in 2012, I had an overwhelming compulsion to put together a book on marriage and forgiveness. Through my own near-divorce experience, I discovered some important keys to what I believe makes a truly successful marriage. It breaks my heart to see so many couples, many in the church, struggling to keep their marriage together or giving up and getting a divorce. It is my hope that this book will reach someone in this situation and change their life the way God has changed mine.

Additionally, this book is written for those that at one time in their life made a decision for Christ but find that they do not have the zeal they once had or have gotten off track with that commitment. I think the two can be related. Usually, if we have troubles in our marriage, it is not the only relationship that is struggling. I wrote this book as a way of organizing my thoughts and sharing what I've learned.

The bonus to repairing a troubled marriage is that as you work to correct the source of the marital problems, you fix the problems that are usually present in your profession or other areas of your life. It is common, especially for men, that when there is chaos at home, there is usually chaos at work. Or when we are unsettled in our marriage, we are unsettled in our job.

The title, *What the Locusts Have Eaten*, is a reference to the second chapter of Joel. Because of the Israelites' sin, God sent drought and locust. The locust destroyed the current crop, and the drought took away a hope for a good crop in the future. But God promised to "repay (or restore) for the years that the locust have eaten" (Joel 2:25, NIV). This is a promise, repeated throughout the Bible, to all that return to God with a humble and broken spirit. When God restores, He does so in a spectacular way. He can make things better than before. He can increase our blessings so the damaged crops are forgotten. God's restoration may or may not look like we envision it. Furthermore, God's timeline is not like ours. In the end, we can be confident that God will do as he says he will do, but we cannot neglect our part. "Even now, declares the Lord, "Return to me with all your heart, with fasting and weeping and mourning."

Rend your heart and not your garments. Return to the Lord your God for he is gracious and compassionate (Joel 2:12–13).

Think about the children of the adult Israelites. The children were experiencing the same lack of food that their parents were. And it was their parents that were being disobedient to God. The children were facing the consequences of the poor decisions of their parents. But as we see throughout the Bible, many times the next generation makes the same choices as their parents. Sometimes the next generation is worse than the previous one. In the same way, divorce will impact not only the children of the couple getting the divorce but many other people as well. Sometimes, the effects of one divorce can be seen generations later.

The locusts are a metaphor for the things that have been destroyed by sin and disobedience. We do things that bring about destruction, and sometimes, these same behaviors have been passed down for generations. We may be the recipient of the consequences of another's bad decisions, but we also pass the consequences of our bad decisions on to our children.

This book is about breaking that cycle or not passing down to future generations a legacy of bitterness, anger, resentment, and unforgiveness. *What the Locusts Have Eaten* is about restoring peace, love, joy, and forgiveness in all areas of your life. It is about having a wonderful and loving, lifelong relationship with your spouse and showing forgiveness and the love of Christ to others as you have been shown.

In 2000 and 2001, I had hit a low point in my life. My twelve-year marriage was about to be over. I had accumulated much debt, and I was having a hard time making ends meet. I was struggling in a less than mediocre job. It was not clear to me at that time exactly how I arrived at where I was. My most dominant emotions were feelings of unfulfilled goals, personal dissatisfaction, and disappointment. My heart was far from God or the things of God. My thoughts were on my own satisfaction and how I had been hurt by others, disappointed by others, and disappointed in myself. I also felt that my life thus far had not come close to my personal expectations of success and happiness.

Divorce was imminent and I welcomed it. Perhaps afterwards I would be able to make some changes, unencumbered by the baggage of the past. I grew up with a self-reliant mind-set, and I was confident that I could make better choices and my situation would eventually improve.

It was then that I met a guy by the name of Dean. Dean felt that he was supposed to start an overcomers group at his church. He advertised his group and tried to get the word out. Dean arrived at the designated meeting spot, every week for six months, and no one had come. Finally, he gave up. He figured it was just not to be for him to have an overcomers group.

Meanwhile, a friend of mine found Dean's group listed on the internet and suggested that I attend. I went to the meeting place the very week that Dean had decided to quit. Not finding anyone there, I called him and he assured me he would be there the following week. We met the next week and every week for the next year or so.

Dean had overcome some of his own poor choices and had made some significant changes in his life. He was trying to help drug addicts and alcoholics through a Christian twelve-step program at his church. Christian from age eleven, I was not averse to having someone to pray with. Even though I had no drug or alcohol issues, I appreciated talking to him about my week, having an accountability partner of sorts. Most of the time, the meetings consisted of just the two of us. Dean's friendship brought a little stability to my chaotic life. About three or four months into our newfound friendship, Dean asked me a simple question. That question changed everything. As I contemplated the answer to his question, it took me down a road I never expected.

As you read this book, I encourage you to take the time to physically write out the answers to the questions at the end of each chapter. I suggest that you get a notebook to record your answers. It will be helpful later. Also, spend plenty of time with each question. Think through each response and try to give as much detail as possible. This works best with an accountability partner or a close confidant that you can be honest and transparent with.

I hope this book blesses you, your marriage, and all of your relationships. Let's begin.

CHAPTER I

WEDDING BELLS

> That is why a man leaves his father and
> mother and is united to his wife, and they become
> one flesh.
>
> —Genesis 2:24 NIV

Think for a moment about the last wedding you witnessed. Maybe your own wedding comes to mind. Perhaps it is the wedding of a close friend or a relative. In the recent past, I have attended a Jewish wedding, a Catholic wedding, a Baptist wedding, and a wedding that had no particular religious affiliation at all. For the most part, each of these weddings were very similar.

Like most weddings, the ones I attended went something like this: Most of the attendees were wearing their Sunday best. There were just shy of two hundred people in attendance. The music played softly in the background and people mingled quietly with each other. The fragrant smell of fresh flowers drifted lightly through the air. An anticipatory buzz filled the room as attendees awaited the entrance of the bride-to-be.

On the podium stood a nervous groom with three of his closest friends, all dressed in tuxedos that made them look sharp and handsome.

Opposite the groomsmen were the friends or sisters of the bride. They were skillfully adorned in matching dresses which they will probably never wear again. The pastor stood in the middle, routinely glancing over his notes.

Then came the bride. The music changed to that familiar tune in which everyone rises to his or her feet in joy and respect. Wow! She looked radiant. Her flowing dress and well-decorated hair made her look like a modern-day princess.

A man, whom I assumed was her father, escorted the bride-to-be down the aisle. I looked to the front row where the man walking to her right would soon be sitting. There seemed to be extra parents. Perhaps I was being cynical, but at that moment I wondered: What if the pastor asked all in attendance if they had ever been divorced or had divorced parents to please stand up? Would the visual make a point to the marrying couple?

What Are They Thinking?

I began to wonder why this soon-to-be married couple thinks they won't end up like so many others. How are they going to be different? Divorced people walked down an aisle like this—happy and elated, making promises to each other in front of a cadre of witnesses. But to what avail? What makes some marriages successful and others not?

I wondered what the groom was thinking then. Was he thinking about how his bride-to-be and he first met? Perhaps he was thinking that if the events of the last year had gone only slightly different, he would not be standing here today. Maybe they would have never met or went on that first date. Was he thinking about what the next five or ten years would bring forth? Was he thinking what a lucky man he was to be marrying such a beautiful, wonderful bride? Perhaps he wasn't thinking much at all, just enjoying the moment and being blissfully happy.

I too wondered what thoughts might be swirling in the bride's mind. Was she thinking about what adventures would unfold as she and her husband's lives unite? She was probably not thinking of dirty diapers, soccer practices, or picking out a new minivan. Most likely, she was excited and nervous and happy—all rolled into one. This was the day she had thought about for a long time, probably since she was a little girl. This was her prince, the man that is perfect for her, and she for him. Was she thinking of why this particular person was best suited for her?

Does this remind you of your own wedding?

Witnessing these weddings certainly spark nostalgic thoughts of my own. At my wedding there were no more than thirty people in attendance, including the wedding party of ten. I was twenty-two years old and my bride was twenty years old when we were married. We thought we knew what we were doing, but in hindsight, we did not have a clue. There were a few people that questioned our wisdom in marrying at such a young age, but that did not deter us. Surprisingly, that chorus was not that loud. We were excited, in love and ready to commit to a lifetime together. I remember wondering what our life would look like in ten, twenty and thirty years.

Divorce

According to the National Center for Health Statistics, there are 2,077,000 marriages a year in the United States. Approximately 1,400,000 of those are first-time marriages. This may be where we get the statistic that half of all marriages end in divorce. I have seen other statistics that suggest a smaller number. Some statistics claim the number of divorces in the United States may be closer to 25 percent or 30 percent.

A common problem with many statistics is that they can be manipulated. When it comes to marriage statistics reporting on successful marriages, one must clearly understand what researchers define as successful. Is a ten-year marriage a success? Is twenty years of being married a success? Some couples get divorced after twenty or more years of marriage. Perhaps the best measure of success is if the marriage remained intact until one partner died. Of course, it would have to be ensured the death was the result of natural causes.

There are many other factors that can skew a statistic, such as the demographics of the sample, the size of the sample, and the representativeness of the sample to the intended population. Population and where someone takes the population from can have a huge impact on the outcome of the statistic though these factors are rarely reported. Suffice it to say, somewhere between 25 and 50 percent of marriages end in divorce. The next logical question is: How or why is this the case? How do we get it so wrong? What happens in the life or mind of a couple that brings them to divorce and many times ill feelings toward each other?

According to one source, the average cost of a wedding is $29,858.[1] It seems to me that you would have to be pretty sure about someone to spend that amount of money on them in one day. How does a couple that is so in love despise each other to the point of divorce just a few years or even a few months later?

As I watch a wedding, I cannot help but wonder where the couple will be in five to ten years. While I hope they will continue to be happily married for as long as they both live, I also consider if the love they feel for each other this day will become hate in a few short years? Will they perpetuate the litany of broken families and one-parent households that are so prevalent today? Will they, years from now, enter the pastor's office for counseling before entertaining the idea of divorce? I want to think that it won't happen, but it might. And it seems that a couple is just as convinced that they need to get a divorce as they were that they were perfect for each other in earlier times.

Can the tragedy of divorce be stopped?

If you are married, think about your own wedding.

- What was your own wedding like?
- What special memories do you have of that day?
- Do you remember your thoughts or hopes or fears?
- Has anything changed?
- If something has changed, what changed and why?

In addition to marriages that end in divorce, there are couples that stay married but one or both partners are extremely unhappy and adversarial. Should this marriage be considered successful? Some married couples stay married for the sake of the children or because

---

[1] https://www.valuepenguin.com/average-cost-of-wedding

a divorce is too costly in a fiscal sense. Some partners stay married because of social stigma and/or family member's potentially adverse reactions. Sundry reasons exist as to why a man and woman remain married even in the midst of great unhappiness without finding a solution to their problem. And the reality is these marriages are just as fractured and dysfunctional as couples that choose to end the marriage through a divorce.

According to the *Journal for Marriage and the Family*, the top three reasons women give for divorce are communication problems, unhappiness, and incompatibility. In most studies, a gaggle of reasons are given for divorce, but they usually start with or are somewhat related to these three. Generally, one person or both people greatly dislike the person they once loved, and now they have no desire to share life with that person, let alone be in the same house with them. How does such a dramatic transformation in one's thinking occur? Or is it a dramatic transformation at all?

So let us consider the happy couple walking down the aisle. Presumably the reason they decided to get married in the first place was they felt they communicated well, were very compatible, and were not only happy but in love. Couples tend to appear, especially on their wedding day, as though their potential reasons for divorce are far away. One must then inquire: If a couple communicates so well before they get married, what changes after marriage? If they are so compatible, what is the cause of becoming incompatible? If they are in love, what changes that feeling to strong dislike or hate? These are the top reasons given for divorce, yet they seem to be a contributing factor for why people get married. How are we making such a flip in our relationships?

Maybe people are getting married for reasons not readily stated and are more self-serving than loving. Do you think it is possible that many of us get married for more selfish reasons and less altruistic motives? The casual observer may conclude that a significant number of divorces seem to be the *result* of purely selfish reasons. Similarly with a closer examination, it would seem that marriage can be based on the same selfish motivations. These reasons we choose the person we do in the first place is entirely self-serving. And when the relationship no longer serves self, people want out of it.

Depending on the source, the percentage of second marriages that end in divorce are between 60 and 80 percent. Wow! One would think that the second time around people would be extra careful to choose a mate and avoid all of the problems they had the first time around.

I almost got divorced. By almost, I mean we were less than a day away from signing the final papers in front of the judge. I could have blamed it on my underdeveloped brain that got me into the marriage in the first place for I have heard many people tell me the reason for their divorce was they were too young when they got married.

However, if you asked me why we were getting a divorce, I would have said we did not have any sustaining mutual love for each other. To put it another way, I felt I was no longer in love with my wife or she with me. And at that time, I certainly *felt* that way. At this crossroad of my life, it is safe to say I was not happy. I wasn't happy with my wife, my job, or myself.

Have you ever heard one or both participants of a troubled marriage say they are no longer "happy" or "in love"? Does it sound a little selfish? Having gone through this exercise, happy to wanting a divorce and then on to a restored marriage, I've given this thought of changing feelings and perspective much thought.

Maybe that person is you. Most people who are on the track for divorce feel this way. Typically, if someone is at this tipping point in their relationship, there was and is definitely a breakdown in good communication. However, counterintuitive as it seems, working on communication issues is secondary. There are primary issues that must be addressed, issues that ultimately are the cause of poor communication and left unaddressed, have the same detrimental effects.

From Love to Divorce

Can divorce be boiled down to a lack of love? Because if one had the same love and desire that he or she had the day they walked down the aisle, there would be no reason for divorce. Do you remember dating your spouse? Do you remember feeling that you would do just about anything for that partner you loved so much? Some of you did crazy things to win the heart or catch the eye of the person you wanted above all others. How do we go from "in love" to "not in love"?

If couples could sustain their wedding day love and admiration, would they ever think of divorce? Is that really the problem regardless of whatever reasons people give for divorce? The by-product of that loveless feeling is one does not act loving toward their spouse, and as a result, a chasm is created between lovers. Soon, each person is hurt from experiencing a withdrawn spouse and unloving interactions with them, and thus, very naturally and instinctively think about self-preservation.

We ultimately all want to be happy, especially in regards to marriage. We even say, "happily married" when we describe a seemingly successful couple. This transfers in our minds and in our functional practice to working toward securing our own happiness in whatever way necessary. We then seek happiness as our goal, stated or not. Does this sound a bit selfish? Not only is it selfish, but if happiness is our goal, we will never reach it.

Think about things that people pursue for happiness and what the outcome is. Some people pursue money as a means to bring them happiness. They always need a little more to reach the goal because what they have is never enough. There are television shows that chronicle the disastrous results of those that have won various public lotteries. We also see examples of people who have amassed wealth in other ways, have the turmoil of their personal lives displayed in mass media.

Many individuals pursue status, positions, or job titles as a way of bringing happiness and contentment to their lives. This also becomes an unsuccessful endeavor. There is always a better position or title and even achieving a particular goal usually does not bring the satisfaction that was imagined.

Should it be any surprise to us that a person cannot bring us happiness either? We can enjoy the company of another and love another. But if our goal is for that person to bring constant happiness and fulfillment to our life, we are likely to be disappointed.

It is said that the worst lie we tell is the one we tell ourselves. When we got married, we were convinced that all of our thoughts were all about the other person. We believed we just wanted to make our partner happy. Were we just fooling ourselves? Were we selfish all along? Maybe we got married for our own happiness and our own benefit and that stuff about being there in sickness and in health, rich or poor, good times and bad were just pretty words.

Is it possible to stay in love with your spouse for the rest of your life? Is it possible to be *happily married*? Is this possible only for a select few? If there really were a secret to a successful marriage, wouldn't someone have told us about it before now? I would think that if someone found the secret, it would be in the headline news.

But maybe the secret is readily overlooked or dismissed. Maybe the secret's potency and effectiveness is hidden to some.

Ask a couple that has been happily married over fifty years what their secret to a long and happy marriage is. They usually say, "We never go to bed angry" or "We are best friends." This sounds like a good advice, but does it really help? It seems a bit simplistic. Is there more? How did they get there? How does a couple become best friends? How does a couple that is married for decades keep from going to bed angry?

Most of us would say that this is what we all want when we walk down the aisle with the love of our life. We want to be best friends with our spouse, and we don't want to get angry with them. Of course, we expect some disagreements but those will be minor.

In the book *Social Animal*, Daniel Goleman tells us of an experiment at Cambridge University on monkeys. The neuroscientist Wolfram Schultz was trying to understand Parkinson's disease. After squirting apple juice in the mouths of monkeys, he would observe a small surge of dopamine in the neurons of the brains of the test monkeys.

After repeatedly giving drinks of apple juice, Schultz observed that the dopamine began to fire just prior to the distribution of the juice. Next, he sounded a tone before administering juice. Soon, the monkeys associated the tone with the arrival of juice. The neurons in the brains of the monkeys began to fire at the sound of the tone instead of the juice. In school, many of us learned about Pavlov's dog salivating at the ringing of a bell in much the same way.

In the same book, another researcher, Read Montague, conducted extensive studies on the human mental system. Montague states that humans construct "anticipatory patterns in our brains to predict the future." An accurate prediction gives us a dopamine squirt as a reward. If our prediction does not match with our reality, there is a problem. In Montague's words, we strive for the harmony between the inner world of our brain—namely our anticipatory predictions—and the outer world of our daily lives—reality experienced. When this harmony is constantly being thwarted, we instinctively attempt to correct it or solve it. Because this phenomenon occurs in all humans, this concept of harmony or disharmony can be applied to marriage. One might project that thwarted anticipatory patterns and the diminishing dopamine delivery is a scientific explanation of what is going on inside our head when our marriage and our partner do not turn out like we expected. Our prediction does not match our reality. And what do we base that expectation on? Usually, our expectation of marriage is based on our culture, our role models in our formative years, and sometimes on television. Is our expectation for marriage based on biblical principles?

For some, there is a disconnection between what we expect marriage to be like and the reality that we experience over time. This is a conflict in our minds. We had a prediction and an expectation and we bought in. Now there are some things that don't add up and do not feel right. When individuals do not highly value the covenant of marriage as an unbreakable promise, the way to solve the aforementioned problem is divorce.

To further compound the factors leading couples toward divorce is the current, predominant culture which teaches and encourages people to constantly seek self-gratifying rewards. For instance, the advertisements we see on television appeal to the personal gratification in our brains. We are, in essence, told via sounds and images that if we buy a certain product, we will be happy and fulfilled in one way or another. The product presents a promise to make us look good or feel good in some way. This is the mentality perpetuated in most areas of our lives. Is it then not only possible but also probable that the same mentality bleeds into one's approach to marriage? Do you think that it is not only possible but probable that we bring the same ideas of consumerism into our marriage?

There is typically frustration when we have a host of relationships in our lives that do not meet our expectations. This list can include: our parents, our kids, our boss, our employees, our friends, and our church. And the list can be long. When we combine unmet expectations with conflict and clashing personalities, the result can easily be a broken relationship.

How does the typical person deal with this frustration? With unmet expectations or anticipations? With decreasing levels of dopamine release? With disharmony with in themselves and without? What do we do when the person we are married to, the person we have knitted our life together with does not fit our expectations of a wife or a husband? What do we do when the anticipatory pattern of a mate and a married relationship that we have mentally constructed is so misaligned that we begin to loathe and despise the very person we have vowed to be with till death do us part?

Perhaps a better question is: How is this problem resolved? How is harmony reestablished? What is the solution when the sight of our mate not only does not produce that dopamine squirt to fire in our brains but also triggers a completely opposite visceral response instead? Is it possible to bring back that loving relationship when we have reached this level? Do we need to change our thinking? Is there a different approach that will make a difference?

First, we must examine where we originally get our individual ideas of what a spouse, child, boss, pastor, friend, and neighbor should be? Does it come from our experiences growing up, observing our parents, friends, others, and even from television and our broader view of culture?

There Is Still Hope

If you are married and don't feel more love for your spouse than on that wedding day, there is hope. If you have not been married but want to have a successful marriage, you can have it. I can honestly say that as each year passes, my wife and I grow closer together and our love deepens. But it certainly was not always that way.

And as I told you, we almost got divorced. As a matter of fact, everyone that knew us then was sure we would get a divorce. I suspect some people were even wondering what took us so long to get divorced. When we announced that we were *not* getting divorced, most people thought we were crazy.

Nevertheless and despite our deeply rooted disharmony (which will be discussed in a later chapter), my wife and I have been married for over thirty years, and I look forward to the future.

My message to you is that there is hope.

You may feel prompted to say, "But you don't know my situation."

My response: it doesn't matter.

You may be thinking, "But I just don't love my spouse anymore."

My response: you can not only love your spouse again but actually love him or her more than when you got married.

For many of us, we called it love when we got married, but it is more closely resembled lust or selfish consumerism and not love at all. The truth is that for many of us, there is a host of things that are out of place. Our relationships have a consumer basis to them. We are looking for fulfillment and happiness in a creation and not the Creator. We have cultivated a lifetime of finding fault, being offended, and not offering forgiveness, and now our marriage is the latest casualty.

Now if you are mumbling that this is impossible, I challenge you to read this book.

1. Commit yourself to digesting and applying the concepts written in these pages to your own situation.

2. Genuinely examine yourself through careful, honest self-evaluation and introspection.
3. Pledge to do the work without preconceived expectations of failure.

In the end, you will be amazed.

There was a time that you pledged to spend the rest of your life with someone. You promised to love, for better or for worse, for richer or for poorer, till death do you part. I hope to share with you the foundational truths—or hidden secret, if you will—that can make that pledge a reality. More than that, I believe that you can grow *with* your spouse, not grow *apart* from your spouse. I am convinced that each year can bring you closer and your love can grow richer.

Questions for Discussion

1. How did you meet your spouse?
2. When and where did one of you propose?
3. What was special or different or memorable about your wedding?
4. What did you like best about your spouse when you first met?

Chapter 2

WHAT IS A MARRIAGE?

So they are no longer two, but one flesh.
Therefore what God has joined together, let no
one separate.

—Matthew 19:6 (NIV)

We have a few significant transitional periods in our lives which are marked by their corresponding events respectively. In some cultures, the transition from childhood to adulthood is a very special time which is given much attention and even a special celebration. Traditional Jews celebrate Bar Mitzvah when a young boy becomes a man or Bat Mitzvah as a young girl becomes a woman. In some African and Indian traditions, this time is an important event as well and is celebrated with much fanfare and tradition. However, the marking of this transitional period has largely been lost in our modern American culture.

A birth of a child or the death of a loved one can be a life-changing moment in one's life. A graduation from college or a retirement from a vocation is a transitional period. We do not graduate and then return to the same class the next semester and start taking notes. We do not retire from a job and then return the next Monday and behave as we did prior.

Another major transitional event in one's life is baptism into Christ. Baptism, generally speaking, is an outward declaration of an inward change. In Christianity, the church celebrates a convert identity change from an enemy of God to having a relationship with God through the blood of Jesus Christ and fullness of the Holy Spirit with the symbolic emersion into water followed by a ceremony. The person that is being baptized relays to those in attendance that they have chosen to follow Jesus Christ and declare Him Lord and Master of their life; and consequently, others can expect a difference in their motives, attitudes, and behavior going forward.

In some instances, this change in one's identity from sinner to saint is also accompanied by a name change. Certainly when we are born, we are given a name, and that name bears meaning. When one's identity changes, it is sometimes deemed appropriate by God for that person to adopt a new name with a new—often better—meaning. In the Bible, there are examples of a few name changes. Some marked a change in relationship to God. Some name changes marked a change in the person's life.

Abram, which means "exalted father" becomes Abraham, which means "father of a multitude." And Sarai, which means "princess" has her name changed to Sarah, which means "noblewoman" when God makes a covenant with Abraham. Other name changes marked a change in relationship to one's purpose and divine calling. Simon becomes Peter, which means "rock" as Peter would be the rock on which Christ built His church. Saul, which means "desired" becomes Paul, which means "humble" as Apostle Paul would spend the rest of his life in humble service to spreading the Gospel of Christ. There are even more examples found in the scriptures.

Another name change occurs when one gets married for the individuals role alters drastically from singleness to unity and oneness with their spouse. Hence, recognition of that identity and relationship change is marked by a name change. The last name of the wife is changed in this major transitional life event. This period of transition from singleness to oneness with another alters one's reality and requires a complete shift in mind-set. For instance, two months before a wedding, a couple usually has different responsibilities and obligations than they have two months after the wedding.

The new couple form a new family. They are now collectively designated by the family name. As new members enter the family, they are part of that family until they repeat the process with someone else to form their own unique family. They are still related to the parents or family they came from, but the relationship and their responsibilities change as they start a family of their own.

Defining Marriage

Have you given much thought to exactly what a marriage is? Until recently, this question was not given much publicity. However, in the last decade or so, the question has been hotly debated by opposing groups with regarding the answer. For thousands of years, in all different cultures, people have been getting married.

Let us consider the practice of marriage. Ever wonder where do our wedding traditions come from? Or how each age and culture practiced marriage?

Legal Contracts

Today in an American culture, marriage is on one level a legal matter. When two people get married, they need a marriage license. Some marriages may include a justice of the peace or a courthouse. Likewise when there is a divorce, there is always a judge involved and usually a couple of lawyers. In biblical times, the Jews required a certificate of divorce, which could only be granted by a judge.

Consider the magnitude of a contract. According to *Merriam-Webster's Collegiate Dictionary*[2], a *contract* is a binding agreement between two or more parties that is legally enforceable.

Why even establish marriage as a legal matter?

To view marriage, an event largely associated with love and good feelings through the aspect of legal enforcement seems awkward and perhaps even distracting of its beauty. Can we legally enforce a marriage? Yet when we get married, we do sign a marriage certificate that is registered with the state. This sort of makes it *feel* like a contract. Thus, is marriage merely a legally enforceable contract?

Is a marriage a legal partnership? *Merriam-Webster's Collegiate Dictionary* describes a *partnership* this way: "a legal relation existing between two or more persons contractually associated as joint principles in a business, a relationship resembling a legal partnership and usually involving close cooperation between parties having specified joint rights and responsibilities."[3] Maybe a marriage is a relationship whereby we cooperate and each have rights and responsibilities. This sounds better than a contract. It may be argued that a marriage has some characteristics of a contract or a partnership.

Yet the mere legality of marriage does not really describe—in fullness—what a marriage is or how it is and ought to be practiced optimally.

Sacred Covenant

A marriage is a covenant between the husband and the wife. How is a covenant different than a contract and why is it important? What are some examples of covenants? The word *covenant* is not one we use often, if at all. In biblical times, the concept of a covenant was much more commonplace than it is in our modern culture. *Merriam-Webster's* definition of a covenant is described as "a formal, solemn and binding agreement. A written agreement or promise *under seal* between two or more parties for the purpose of some action."[4] A wedding is a formal event where we make a solemn promise to each other and God. As a result, the marriage is sealed by God. The promise is the vows we make each other. The performance or action is the marriage and the joining of two lives.

A covenant is a binding arrangement or agreement between two or more parties that forms the foundation of their relationship. The binding of the parties is permanent. The essence of a covenant is that it is an unbreakable promise. The only exit from a covenant is the death of one of the participants.

Historically, a covenant involved sacrifices, witnesses and a promise. The covenant promise usually had a symbol attached to it as a reminder to those involved in the covenant.

In Genesis 15:9–17, we see the ritual known as "cutting a covenant." This ritual involves cutting one or more animals in half. The halves are laid on the ground apart. Then the parties entering into covenant with each other would walk between the halved sacrifices.

They were saying in effect that if they failed to keep their part of the agreement, they deserved the same fate as the animals. When we get married, we usually do not sacrifice animals and walk between them. (It may help us take the vows a bit more seriously.)

The basis of a covenant is that it is an unbreakable promise. In a covenant, a person says that even though situations may change and feelings, circumstances and other things may change in the future, what the other party can count on is that the promise made that day will hold true. Does this have a ring of familiarity to it? The officiator of a wedding usually asks if each person agrees to remain married for better or worse, richer or poorer, in sickness or in health.

The vows that are exchanged at a wedding are the promises that the couple make to each other. They pledge how they are sacrificing themselves for the other in this new arrangement. The essence of each vow is how this promise and this new arrangement is going to benefit the other to the sacrifice of the one making the promise. Think about that for a moment. In the last chapter, it was pointed out that many times we view the marriage and relate to one another in a marriage as a consumer. However, the covenant promise is for the other's benefit, not our own. Why else would we declare to be counted on as faithful regardless of the circumstances or what may come our way? What other reason would we state that until we die, we will stay true to a promise we make on that day?

We have witnesses in attendance at weddings, not just to show off our good fortune for having found a mate but to attest to the fact that we made the promises that we have made. These witnesses are in attendance as a requirement of the covenant.

Finally, before the officiator of the wedding pronounces that the covenant is complete, we exchange rings as a daily reminder of the covenant promise that we made on that day. Like the rainbow in the sky after a rain reminds us of God's promise not to destroy the earth again with water, our rings reminds us of the covenant promise we made on our wedding day to our spouse.

The Difference: Benefit vs. Promise

An important difference between a contract and a covenant is the concept of benefit versus promise. In entering into a contract, we are usually not concerned with how the contract benefits the other party. If I sign a contract to buy a house from someone, my concern is not that they receive the best deal possible regardless of how it affects me. On the contrary, my objective in purchasing a house would be to get the maximum benefit for the lowest price. Such is the case with any contract. My motivation is to look out for my own best interest, and I expect the opposing party is aiming to do the same.

In contrast, when one enters into a covenant, the emphasis is on the unbreakable promise. The important point of the covenant is that come what may, the promise the participants are making will hold true.

In the Bible, we read in Genesis 9 of the first recorded covenant that God tells Noah that He will never again destroy mankind with water. God gives us a rainbow as a symbol of His covenant with us.

In Exodus, God makes a covenant with Abraham. God's covenant with Abraham was sealed with the covenant sign of circumcision. Circumcision was the symbol of God's covenant with Abraham and his descendants. When God made a covenant with the Israelites in Exodus 31:16–17, it was sealed with the Sabbath as a holy day of rest. The symbol of God's covenant with the Israelites was the Sabbath. They rested on that day as a reminder of God's covenant with them.

In Mark 14:24, Jesus tell the disciples that the cup of wine represents His blood of the new covenant that is poured out for many. When we take communion, we eat the bread and drink the wine. These elements are symbols of the new covenant we have with God through the blood of Christ. We have the promise of eternal life through the blood of Christ.

Expectations and Enemies of the Promise

If I interview with a perspective employer for a job, I want to know what I will be doing and what is expected of me. Before I agree to be employed, I want to understand as best as I can what I am signing up for. The fundamental understanding of what is expected of me and what my duties and responsibilities are is the basis of our mutual relationship going forward. If I or my employer have a disagreement or misunderstanding, we can go back to what we established in the beginning.

It is important to understand what a covenant is because it establishes what we can expect and what we cannot expect from our spouse. If we recognize that the marriage began when we made a promise to love in good times and bad, we know that we can expect we won't always be pleased with current events in our lives. In comprehending what a covenant is, we know that the goal of the relationship is not our personal happiness. We did not say, "I agree to remain married to you as long as I am happy and satisfied." The goal is therefore not eternal bliss for each of the party. The goal is to honor, respect, and to love and serve each other in a unique relationship that helps us to grow and mature as we mimic Christ.

When we do not understand that a marriage is a covenant, and what a covenant is, we default to the thinking of benefit and reward. We then look for our needs being met and our continual fulfillment as the foundation for how we will act toward our spouse. It is critical that we have an understanding of what a marriage is, what the goal is, and what we should and should not expect in a marriage.

It seems that on the surface, it is the concept of personal benefit that we sometimes mistakenly apply to a marriage. Is it possible that our view of marriage as a contract or a partnership, and our understanding of them, confuses us to the concept of what a marriage truly is? Additionally, could that mental mislabeling be a factor in what we expect and anticipate when we enter into a marriage?

We have laws in place to protect us. If there were no traffic laws, driving across town during rush-hour would be a challenge to say the least. Our state and national laws cannot prevent a wrongdoing, but they discourage it and establish the consequences if someone breaks them. God's laws are much the same. We benefit from keeping them. We are not forced to keep God's laws, but we are better off for it.

Disobedience, Violations of the Covenant Detracts from or Denies Us the Promise

Living together before getting married violates God's law. We can do it, but it will not be in our best interest. Among other things, this arrangement is based on personal feelings and satisfaction. If one person feels their needs are not met or they are no longer receiving the acceptable level of personal enjoyment from the arrangement, they can just leave. The consequence being that this mentality is then the basis of the relationship when one does get married. The arrangement of being together before marriage then feeds our needs and wants approach after we become married. This makes it more difficult to view marriage the way it is intended.

This then is how we should view marriage. It is a solemn promise to each other and God that we will do all that we say we will. We are committed to each other. We will have fellowship with each other, and we will share our lives with each other. The first step in beginning a marriage or saving a troubled one is to remind ourselves that we have made a covenant promise to each other. The basis of a marriage is a covenant promise. It is not a contingent promise based on our continual satisfaction or our personal enjoyment or happiness. The covenant promise is the promise to remain married regardless of what comes our way or what obstacles we face. We commit to our partner and the marriage is that commitment. Happiness is not the goal of a covenant. This goal is self-defeating anyway.

At first glance, the idea of remaining married because of a promise seems a little cold and unromantic. On the contrary, it is one of the most loving and selfless things someone can do. It is truly an act of love to pledge to be there for another no matter what may come your way. We see this when we watch a wedding and the person officiating the wedding rattles off a list of good and bad scenarios. The thought of these two people saying they are committed to the marriage and the covenant is the picture of love. But then when we do not feel the acceptable level of personal happiness, we look for the exit. It is a universal truth that if in any endeavor you make happiness a goal, you will never reach it. However, when we make God our goal, the by-product is fulfillment.

Paradigm Shift

Some may try to minimalize the marriage covenant to make its dissolution easier to accept. The only real dissolution of a covenant is death. This is why the marriage vows end with "till death do us part." The death of one member of the covenant ends the covenant, not the dissatisfaction of one or both.

The problem is that we many times view a marriage as an agreement to meet one another's needs and make each other happy. When that fails to happen on a regular basis, we look to end the marriage so we can find another that is up to the task. This is really an impossible assignment. You cannot find someone who will constantly keep you happy and your needs fulfilled. The answer is to look to God. When we work on developing a deeper relationship with God and focus on Him as the center of our life, our perspective changes. At the center of every divorce is a heart issue. When our heart is in the wrong place, problems follow. Where your heart is, there your treasure will be also.

Let us start with the understanding that two people have made an unbreakable promise to each other. They have walked through the middle of the halved animals and sealed the promise with matching rings before God and witnesses. Having the thorough understanding of a marriage being a unique covenant relationship is important. It establishes the sincerity of the promise that we have made, and it puts the focus of the relationship on commitment and self-sacrifice and not benefit, reward, and satisfaction.

This is a difficult concept to embrace because the concept of covenant is not something that we are familiar with. Benefit, reward, looking out for self and pleasure seeking is something we are inanely familiar with.

I know there are many people that do not seem to take marriage that serious. This may be why divorce is such an epidemic in our culture. Start here. Make the commitment to work on growing in this covenant and growing with your partner in mutual love and fellowship and the sharing of your lives.

I understand that there may be many different people reading this book. Some may be newly married couples that wish to start their journey on the right foot. I commend you on your foresight. There may also be couples on the brink of divorce that do not think it is possible to love that spouse again. Quite honestly, some may be reading this for clues on how to get the next one right. For you I will say, "There isn't a next one." You are with the person you are with for a reason. You chose your spouse and God blessed the union.

Perhaps you think I do not understand your situation and some of this doesn't apply to you. It is too late. There has been too much hurt or distrust. I promise you that I have heard or said many of the same excuses that you can think up.

When I decided to call off the divorce proceedings that I had initiated, I really thought it was probably too late. This belief was reinforced when my wife said she would file for divorce instead. She also told me she was finally over it, and that unless God Himself told her to stay married, it wasn't happening. At this time, we had been separated for about a year and the marriage was a mess. Not only was there not a shred of trust left, but the prospect of putting the pieces back together seemed a bigger job than just starting over with someone else. Our marriage was hopeless. I remember thinking that even if by some miracle we stayed married, it would be a daily chore with no true love and we could never undo the damage that was done. I am happy that this was not the case. Yes, the first several months were difficult because of our previous behaviors. But by having a change of heart and mind, true relationship was the end result.

Whatever your reasons are for a troubled marriage, I ask that you temporarily put them aside. Forget for a moment who is at fault and who did what. Forget about lies and hurts and infidelities. Forget about the lack of love or companionship or whatever the issues you feel are most pressing. We will address those things later in the book.

For now, however, put all of that aside. For now focus on two things. First, at one point in time, you loved the person that you made a covenant with. You loved that person more than anything and wanted to spend your life with them. Second, if you do not fix the true problem, your chances are greater that you will get divorced again with the next spouse. Why not just fix the marriage you are already in and make it better than you could have ever imagined?

Questions for Discussion

1. What were the vows you recited at your wedding?
2. What are your thoughts on the concept of a covenant?

CHAPTER 3

THE GROWING YEARS

> If anyone causes one of these little ones—
> those who believe in me-to stumble, it would be
> better for them to have a large millstone hung
> around their neck and to be drowned in the
> depths of the sea.
>
> —Matthew 18:6 (NIV)

Consider a classroom full of second-grade children, energetic seven-year-olds. These children seem to have great potential. If one were to ask them what they want to be when they grow up, their responses may range from ballerina to basketball star and from fireman to doctor. Let us suppose that the children in this second-grade class represent a mixture of all different ethnic and cultural backgrounds. Additionally, present in the class are a variety of socioeconomic levels.

Evidenced in the room, each little brain full of activity has a distinct personality. Some like to talk, others are a bit shy. Some children follow along in their book as the teacher reads and others seem to be counting the patterns on the ceiling tiles. Despite their unique personalities and talents, the biggest predictor of future success for these children is not whether they are rich or poor. It is not whether they are gregarious or shy. The biggest predictor of their future success is whether or not they grow up in a loving two-parent household or not.

The Effects of Divorce on Children

Contrary to widely held public opinion, children of divorced parents are not likely to be "just fine." Frequently stated rationale for divorce, "the children will be happier when their parents are happier," was proven wrong in light of published statistics and studies. Certainly, a happy, pleasant environment will have positive influence on children. However, research seems to point to greater benefit for the child when parents remain married. And if being honest, the adults seeking divorce are usually thinking less about the child and more about themselves.

Identity and self-worth. Generally speaking, individuals think of themselves in accordance with what the most important person in their life thinks of them. Similarly, children internalize what people think of them by what is said to them and about them and by actions, observed or experienced. A child automatically assesses the information passing through their five senses and interprets or decodes their meaning. For instance, a parent can tell their child "I love you" and make all manner of promises. But if that same parent does not fulfill those promises and frequently yells and screams at the child, before long the child will reconcile the words "I love you" with actions that bring hurt and heartache. Furthermore they may choose to be equally suspicious of other things that the parent tells them. The words are not what will win out; rather the actions and the emotions that are associated with those actions will attach themselves to certain words and devoid them of meaning or alter their true meaning. If the parent's words and actions do not match, the child is likely to develop a posture to relationships where they feel they cannot rely on others and must rely on themselves.

Schema and attachment. An infant or a child is constantly recording the world around them. Among other things, they are establishing a sense of trust or mistrust about the world based on interactions with those that took care of them. Adults sometimes mistakenly think their actions will not adversely affect their children. Some believe that some counseling or gifts will correct any damage done by a divorce.

Swiss philosopher and psychologist Jean Piaget developed what is know as the Piaget Stages of Cognitive Development. According to this theory, children must reach a particular stage before they are able to perform certain tasks or understand certain concepts. Piaget's forth stage is 11 years old and older. Piaget says that this is the stage when we develop theoretical, hypothetical, counterfactual thinking, abstract logic and reasoning. This is the age at which we try to make sense of the world around us and we think and reason about our inter-actions with our caregivers and how we fit into our environment.[2]

In adolescence, past memories are reinterpreted and recon-structed in creative ways. Even small slights from childhood, real or imagined, can become huge past offenses to the teenaged mind. With their newly acquired mental skills, the adolescent mind puts together and tries to make sense of events and actions from their past. The teen may become resentful and angry at their parents for reasons the parent does not understand. And that is in an ordinary, functional two-parent family. Add to this a divorce and all of the hurt and drama that comes with it, and it spells trouble.

Shame and blame. In addition to this, teenagers are effected by what David Elkind in his book, *The Hurried Child*, calls imaginary audience. In essence, it is what most parents of a teenager already knows. They think everyone is looking at them. This explains why teenagers have such a strong reaction to the divorce or separation of their parents. To the teenaged mind, everyone knows all about the sordid details of their parent's divorce, and they are embarrassed and humiliated. The blame for this embarrassment and humiliation is usually the parents. Given our social media-drenched world, many personal details are even more public than they were decades ago. Depending on the age of the child and other circumstances, the child may, for a time, blame themselves for the divorce of their parents.

---

[2]   https://www.pschologynoteshq.com/piagetstheory

Rushing Childhood

The concept of divorce rushing childhood is detailed in a 1981 book by David Elkind titled *The Hurried Child*.[3]

Divorce rushes the child's childhood. It robs them of carefree kid like fun and adventures and forces them to interact more with the adults in their lives and less with their own peers. This is especially true when the parent turns to the child or teen for emotional support or to win the arguments they can't win with their former spouse. The parent may look to the child as a confidant. Many times a divorced or separated parent will turn to the child or teen as a partner in the decision-making process. All of this disrupts the natural-growing process and the natural role that the child plays in their growth development. It forces them to think about adult things and adult circumstances and takes away from the feelings of security and safety. In the end, this is likely to lead to resentment of the parent for their actions.

Below are some shocking statistics about children of divorce compiled by Larry Bilotta in the late '90s. The statistics have not improved since then.

> Forty percent of children growing up in America today are being raised without their fathers. (Horn and Busy 1997)

> Children from divorced homes have more psychological problems than homes that have encountered death. (Robert E. Emery 1988)

> Studies conducted in the early 1980's demonstrated that children in repeat divorces earned lower grades then their counterparts,

---

[3] The Hurried Child, Growing up too fast, Addison-Wesley Publishing Company Reading, Massachusetts. Menlo Park, California. London Amsterdam. Don Mills, Ontario. Sydney.1981

and their peers rated them as less pleasant to be around. (Cherlin 1981)

Teenagers in single-parent families and in blended families are three times more likely to need psychological help within a given year. (Hill 1993)

Children from divorced homes have more psychological problems than children from homes disrupted by deaths. (Emery 1988)

A child in a female-headed home is ten times more likely to be beaten or murdered. (Amneus 1984)

Children from broken homes are almost twice as likely to attempt suicide as those who do not come from broken homes. (Velez-Cohen 1988)

Children of divorced parents are roughly two times more likely to drop out of high school than peers who live with non-divorced parents. (McLanahan and Sandefur 1994)

The point is this: when a couple is thinking about divorce, they may be ignorant of these statistics concerning the potential, even likely outcomes of their children. Another possibility is that they are not ignorant at all but steeped in self-deception and self-justification, reasoning that their children will be "just fine" or even "better off." Yet in reality, their thoughts are really on themselves and not on the children at all.

In light of these statistics, it is hard to make the argument that children of divorce will be "just fine" or "better off." Divorce affects the children in a dramatic way. Children from divorced homes have greater rates of suicide, psychological problems, and lower grades in school. They are at a greater danger of beatings or deaths. These should be sobering statistics. Did you read the line that said children are less devastated by death than by divorce? That alone should cause one to pause when considering divorce.

It is important to acknowledge that not *every* child from a divorced family is doomed to failure. Some can go on to be a very successful adult. The important point is that many times, significant problems can be the result of the divorce. When considering a divorce, consider also that there are likely to be sundry consequences that can reveal themselves in the aftermath, sometimes many years down the road. Furthermore, the propensity for children to divorce in their marriage increases. The cycle can continue for generations.

This is the bottom line: there is no evidence that a divorce will have no lasting effect on children.

The Congressional Record H3814 reports the following story: A few years ago, a greeting card company offered free cards to inmates from a prison to send to mothers on mother's day. Nearly all of the prisoners took the offer and sent cards to their mothers. So the greeting card company was somewhat encouraged by the success and decided they would make the same offer when father's day rolled around. They offered free cards to send to fathers on father's day. They had zero takers. There was not one person in the prison that wanted even a free card to send their father on father's day. (http://thomas.loc.gov/cgi-bin/query/R?r109:FLD001:H53814 website: Congress.Gov, reference H3814).

This is obviously an indictment in regard to fatherlessness and those that end up in prison. I think it would not be a stretch, given the statistics sited above, to expect most, if not all, of the prisoner's parents were divorced.

Interconnectedness

As part of a greater community, we all touch the lives of many other people. Your life is connected to friends, coworkers, relatives, and acquaintances at church and other places you spend your time. Because we are "caught in a web of interconnectedness and mutuality," our actions have far reaching effects and influences perhaps tens or more likely hundreds of other people (Martin Luther King Jr.). Be it a successful marriage or a divorce, both touch lives that we may not even be aware of. We often have no idea who is observing form a distance and what influence our actions have on them. Thus, let us be encouraged to weigh our actions and all of their consequences carefully and thoughtfully.

This information is not aimed to produce guilt or shame. People cannot be guilted or shammed into staying married. The purpose, rather, is to demonstrate the absolute seriousness and destruction of divorce. The hurt and consequences produced as a result of divorce affect many people for many years to come, even beyond one's own lifetime. Divorce can have a ripple effect for multiple generations.

Before going down the road of divorce, consider that maybe there is another answer. Consider what your marriage would look like if hurt feelings and a destructive relationship was transformed into a loving, compassionate, and forgiving relationship. Consider that fixing a broken marriage can also have an effect on many people for generations to come.

When we are an infant, our atmosphere and surroundings, loving touch or lack thereof, all gets recorded and translated. Stresses and emotions are felt and processed. In the early growing years, these same variables and more are added to the mix, and we are more cognizant of them. We form opinions of ourselves and others, and the translated messages may begin to be reflected outwardly. Then the teenage years where we try to put it all together and formulate a presentation of who we are as a distinctive individual. The whole process is extraordinary and unique to each individual. There is such a myriad of influences and stimuli that we interpret and process and react to from birth to late teen. It all builds on itself.

Each person on this earth has a totally personal set of experiences that are unique to them. How we react, what we believe about ourselves and others, our experiences, and our fears and reservations all combine into the hopper that makes up each of us. Then we go out into our community and world and take this hidden DNA with us. Usually, we look for a partner to replicate the process with; a partner that has their own unique variables. The best outcome is if we can pass on the better things, we have learned and experienced and end the cycle of passing on the less desirable lessons or experiences to those in our care.

How do we do this? How do we help those in our care or circle of influence to themselves have a good outcome when we don't have the answer for ourselves? How do we teach our children to have a good marriage when ours falls apart? Do we just tell them not to do what we did? What did we do that brought the result it did?

In the first and second chapter, I talked about how sometimes we get married for our benefits, wants, and needs and not truly the other person. And in the divorce mode, the person we are thinking most about is ourselves, not children and certainly not the spouse.

Isn't this the exact opposite of what Jesus taught? Read chapters 5, 6, 7, and 8 of Matthew. How do these chapters line up with putting ourselves first? And if it doesn't line up, then what does that reveal about the condition of our heart? What does that say about where we are spiritually?

This book is about marriage, but it is also about living a God-centered life. It is about not just having a successful marriage but having a successful life. I'm not talking about success in terms of money or things. To me, a successful life is one that points others to Christ and in which I know I am doing His will.

When our marriage is a train wreck, usually other areas of our life is or soon will be as well. The opposite is true. When our marriage is healthy because we have our heart right, the other areas of our life seem to be working as well.

The same concepts I talk about to fix a broken marriage works to fix the other areas of one's life that is broken as well.

Questions for Discussion

1. When you were young, what did you want to be when you grew up?
2. Try to list the people that your marriage touches.
3. What is your relationship with your father like and why?
4. What is your relationship with your mother like and why?
5. Was it always that way? When did it change?
6. What was the most memorable thing during your childhood—good and bad?

CHAPTER 4

FORGIVENESS FROM OTHERS

> Therefore, if you are offering your gift at the
> altar and there remember that your brother or
> sister has something against you, leave your gift
> there in front of the altar. First go and be recon-
> ciled to them; then come and offer your gift.
> —Matthew 5:23–24

Leave Your Gift

In the fifth chapter of Matthew, Jesus gives this instruction. He tells us that if we are offering our gift at the altar or worshiping and focusing on God and someone comes to mind that has something against us, we are to stop what we are doing and seek reconciliation. Then we can return to presenting our gift or worshiping.

Many times, we are very cognizant of those who have wronged or offended us. And we will address that in the next chapter. But it seems that we do not spend adequate time considering who may have something against us. We may brush it aside or minimize it. We may justify our behavior or consider that the other person is the true source of the offense. But Jesus tells us to seek out someone that has something against us and make it right.

If you have ever had a couple of children in your care that were misbehaving, the words of Jesus make sense. Suppose you have two children, Jack and Jill. Let's say that Jack is having one of those days. Jack is upset about something, and he decides to act out toward his sister, Jill. Jack pulls Jill's hair, pushes her down, and takes her toy. A short time later, Jack is feeling better and isn't thinking about how he acted toward Jill. Jack comes to you with a smile and a hug and is looking for the same. But before you can give Jack the love and affirmation he is looking for, you want him to go and make things right with his sister. Why would that change just because we are older? I think this is sort of what Jesus is saying here. God wants to have a relationship with us. But before we get into worship and communicating, He wants us to make sure we don't have some unfinished business with a brother or a sister.

As parents, we ask our children to reconcile with each other when they have a conflict. Why? One reason may be that it restores the relationship between the siblings. If the conflict remains unresolved, it is likely to get in the way of their relationship with the parent. It makes sense to me that God wants the same thing for us. Jesus tells us that we are to be reconciled to our brother or sister, then we have a clear mind to worship God.

Humility

A hallmark of humility is putting others first. The act of putting others first is not our default setting. Instinctively, we usually look out for and protect number one. We seek self-preservation and self-promotion and don't always consider others before ourselves. But in God's kingdom, putting others first is one of the things we are called to do. With Christ as our example, we are to humbly consider others first.

Many places in the Bible, the first step in the restoration process is to humble oneself. That may be because it is the opposite of humility, pride, that usually gets us in to trouble in the first place. The Bible says, "If my people that are called by my name will humble themselves" (2 Chron. 7:14). Over and over again, we get the formula to humble ourselves, pray and seek God. It is oneself in the proper order. Then we can move forward with putting other things back in place.

If I go to someone and clear up anything they may have against me, then I am doing what I can to not be the stumbling block to them in their relationship with God. I do not want to be the reason someone else may have struggles. And how can I help a brother if I am the person that is a hindrance?

In Matthew chapter five, Jesus asks us to consider who we may have offended and essentially to stop worshiping until we have tried to reconcile with that person. Thinking about who we may have offended is just as important, maybe more, than thinking about who may have offended us.

Vinny

I'd like to tell you the story of Vinny (not his real name). In the mid '70s, Vinny was about nine years old. Vinny's parents had some personal issues, and they were separated. Vinny lived with his dad who was a verbally abusive alcoholic. Vinny lived with his dad because between the two, he was the better parent. When things got bad with Vinny's dad, the state would remove him from the home and put him in foster care. At the age of nine, Vinny had been in and out of foster care several times.

On one of those forays into foster care, Vinny met Jack (not his real name). Vinny and Jack were the same age. Jack's parents sometimes took in foster children. And when Vinny was removed from his dad's house, he went to live with Jack and his family.

Jack was a jerk toward Vinny. For most of the six months or so that Vinny lived with him, Jack was mean and sometimes cruel. Eventually, Vinny went back to his dad's house, and the relationship between Vinny and Jack was over.

As the years passed and Jack got older, he thought about Vinny from time to time. Jack changed from those early years and many times prayed for Vinny as he came to mind. He had hoped that Vinny's life improved, but he really had no idea how things had turned out.

In 2017, Jack participated in a men's accountability group at his church. On one occasion when he met with his accountability partner, Jack relayed the story of Vinny. He was thinking about this verse in Matthew 5:23, and he asked his accountability partner if he thought he should write Vinny a letter. Jack reasoned that it may not be a good idea to open old wounds with someone forty years later. It was certainly a rough time in Vinny's life, and he probably didn't want to be reminded of it.

Jack's accountability partner said he should write the letter.

Jack then argued that he could write Vinny a letter but not include a return address. He claimed that Vinny could be in a bad way and providing him with an address may not be a safe thing to do.

Jack's accountability partner said he should provide a return address so that Vinny could have the opportunity to respond.

Jack sent the letter. He was not certain he had the right person or address. He told Vinny that he was sorry for the mistreatment so many years ago. He said that at a time when Vinny needed to be shown love and compassion and kindness that he did not get it from him. Jack told him that he would act differently today, but he did not when he should have. Jack asked Vinny for forgiveness and signed the letter.

Eight days later came a response in the mail. Vinny said, "Yes, you have the right person, and I have been looking for you."

Jack said he felt ashamed and remorseful as he prepared himself for what might come next. He knew that he deserved whatever Vinny had to say about the way Jack acted toward him and what effect it may have had.

Vinny went on to say that he had forgiven Jack years ago. He was happy to get the letter and wanted to know how Jack and his family were doing. He wanted to thank Jack's parents for taking him in and caring for him when he needed it most.

Jack and Vinny exchanged phone numbers and caught up on the events of the years. Jack said he could hear the love of Christ in Vinny's voice. He knew that Vinny had truly forgiven him and there was no resentment in him.

We all need forgiveness from someone. We sometimes offend others and may not be aware of it. Sometimes we offend or hurt others and we are painfully aware of it. When we are aware of it, Jesus tells us to do what we can to make it right. We are to reconcile with the other person.

Who Is the Judge?

I put forgiveness from others first in the section on forgiveness because I think we need to examine our own behavior first. Before we even consider the behavior of someone else, we should first consider how we may have hurt or offended others.

I think sometimes I must mess up several times a day. I don't say the right thing or respond the way I should. Maybe I react crossly or seem uncaring when I should have taken time to think about how Jesus would want me to respond.

And when I think of my past interactions with others, my transgressions seem to mount up fairly quickly. I think we are all inclined to judge our own offenses much less harshly than we judge the offenses of others toward us. In a like manner, we tend to be much more dismissive and forgiving of errors by someone we have a favorable opinion of and less so of someone we don't.

We may keep a mental tally of the offenses of others, but do we keep a mental tally of our own infractions?

Our Impact on Others

We all can have both positive and negative impact on others that we come in close contact with as we navigate through life. The focus here is to think about who you may have impacted in a negative way and so your best to change that. If we were truly peacemakers as we interacted with others, we can make a difference in their life as well as our own. We may not be able to erase in the mind of someone else a negative emotion they have toward us for a past event; however, it is incumbent for us to try. The goal is for all to experience the freedom of forgiveness. We want everyone to know God, to experience forgiveness for themselves, and to extend that same forgiveness to someone else.

Helping Others Heal

If you have offended someone or hurt them, you can either ignore it and allow that offense to grow and become a problem for them and you. Or you can try to restore the relationship and benefit both them and you. When we go to the person that has something against us, we help them heal and we help ourselves. The goal is to imitate Christ's love for others and to point others to God. We do this when we care that someone has something against us, and we do what we can about it.

Questions for Discussion

1. Who may have something against me and why?
2. Is there someone that I avoid?
3. Who do I know that would not give me a good reference to others and why?

CHAPTER 5

FORGIVENESS

Be kind and compassionate one to another,
forgiving each other, just as in Christ God forgave you.

—Ephesians 4:32

In her book, *Unbroken*, Laura Hillenbrand tells the story of Louis
Zamperini, a World War II Army Air Forces bomber who was adrift
in the Pacific Ocean for forty-seven days. When he finally reaches
land, it is only to fall into the hands of the enemy, the Japanese army.
The book chronicles the unimaginable torture that Louis endures at
the hands of a sadistic guard the prisoner's nickname, the Bird.

Years later when Louis is rescued and back home, he cannot
escape the nightmares of his time in captivity. His life is spiraled
out of control with anger and alcoholism. It is after he becomes a
Christian at a Billy Graham tent revival and learns about forgiveness
that his life is changed.

The highlight of the book is when Louis Zamperini has an
opportunity to confront the Bird. Unsure if the meeting will take
place, Louis writes out a letter to the Bird describing the stress and
humiliation he felt during the time under his discipline. Louis
describes the hate he had for his captor. Then Louis tells him that
because of Jesus, he now forgives him and prays for him.

Louis Zamperini's forgiveness of the man that tortured and
humiliated him can only be explained through the power of the Holy
Spirit.

What about forgiving someone that hurts those we love? On October 2, 2006, at the West Nickel Mines School in West Nickel, Pennsylvania, a milk truck driver by the name of Charlie Roberts walked into the one-room schoolhouse with a loaded gun. Charlie told the twenty-six children that he was sorry for what he was about to do. He is quoted in news reports to have said he was angry at God and needed to punish some Christian girls to get even with Him.

In 1997, Charlie's wife, Amy, gave birth to their first child. The baby girl died twenty minutes after being born. For almost nine years, Charlie let the anger at God for the death of his daughter fester inside of him. Charlie was at the Amish school to kill some Christian girls as retaliation against God for the death of his baby daughter.

Before the first shot rang out, a thirteen-year-old girl by the name of Marian said, "Shoot me first."

We do not know why Marian would make such a request. Maybe because she knew in her heart she was ready to meet her maker. Maybe she figured a bullet for her would be one less for someone else. She may have felt that it was her duty to protect the younger children that were present. We cannot know for certain why she shouted such a selfless statement. When the police broke into the school, they found ten girls shot. Marian was one of the girls that was killed. In the end, Charlie had turned the gun on himself to end his own life.

The story does not end there. Within hours, the Amish were expressing forgiveness toward Charlie Roberts for what he had done. The same day, the Amish neighbors visited the Roberts's family to comfort them in their grief. Yes, the Amish went to the home of the man that had killed their innocent children to comfort his wife and family in *their* time of grief. This is what forgiveness looks like.[4]

If we are honest, our first reaction is that we could never forgive someone that daily tortured us and beat us. Furthermore, even if we could forgive someone that hurt us, it is another level to forgive

---

[4] Book Amish Grace, How Forgiveness Transcended Tragedy, Donald B. Kraybill, Steven M. Nolt, David L. Weaver-Zercher, 1st edition, published by Jossey-Bass, A Wiley Imprint, San Franscisco, CA., 2007

someone that hurts or kills our children. But we are called to forgive as God has forgiven us. Truthfully, we hold on to offenses and do not offer forgiveness for things that pale in comparison to these two examples. I think maybe we view the phrase "as God has forgiven you" in the context of to the extent of which I have sinned. In other words, maybe we think I can forgive someone of lying to me because I lied to someone else before. Or I can forgive someone of being a jerk because I have acted like a jerk. But I cannot forgive someone of a horrible act that I have never done or would never do. This is a self-pious way of looking at forgiveness. The human heart is evil and capable of just about anything. In considering levels of offense and degrees of sin, we usually minimize our own sins and offenses and find the offenses of others much more inexcusable. The truth is that we all owed a debt we could not pay. The Bible tells us that all sin separates us from God.

My wife and I bought our first house in Orlando when we were in our mid-twenties. It was a small two-bedroom house on half of an acre of land. We were so excited to have a house of our very own. We bought the house from an elderly lady whose husband built it himself when they were much younger. Because the previous owner carried the note, no inspections were required by the lender.

We were not very knowledgeable about home ownership and everything that it entailed. I was not very handy, and this house presented plenty of opportunity to hone those skills. One day, we began to notice that the drains seemed to empty much too slowly. Additionally, the toilet did not seem to be in optimal working order. My neighbor suggested to me that I may have a problem with my drain field. I had no idea what he was talking about. I soon received an education as to exactly how a septic tank, drain field, and leech bed worked.

It turns out that when I flushed the toilet or put something down the sink, it did not travel to a far off receptacle through a series of tunnels and ducts, never to be seen again. Our refuse went into a large cement tank (septic tank) that was buried in my yard. As the water level in the septic tank rises to a certain level, it then passes out through one of four or so conduits (drain field) on the opposite end of the tank.

In present day, these conduits are usually made of a thick plastic that is perforated on the part that faces down. Because the house I owned was much older, my drain field was constructed of curved terracotta tiles buttressed together. At the end of these fingers, the waste water continues out to an area of soil and rocks (leech field) beneath the surface. There, the processed waste water disseminates further into the ground.

Prior to this time, I had no knowledge of septic systems and how they operated. I was not aware of the need to have a septic system inspected when purchasing a residence that has one.

In addition to my lack of knowledge in matters of sewage removal, I was not very knowledgeable about plants and trees. I did not recognize the interesting tree about six feet above the roof line as a Dwarf Holly bush. Additionally, I did not know that the tall tree was precisely over the part of the yard that contained the curved terracotta conduits. I soon discovered that the roots of this Dwarf Holly had found their way between the terracotta and grew as fat as the tunnel itself.

Unforgiveness

There is not just one tunnel that goes out toward the leech bed. There are usually three to five. Maybe this is so that if one becomes a problem, the others will continue to do the job, temporarily. In my case, all of the tunnels were either filled with roots or totally collapsed.

It occurred to me that this is precisely the way unforgiveness and bitterness works in our lives. When someone or something offends us and we do not show true, honest forgiveness, it is a root that has just worked its way into our spiritual drain field. At first, it may be small, even undetectable. However, given time and fertilizer, this root will grow. In the beginning stages, water continues to flow by the small root. This root isn't even a problem; it is an annoyance at best. But the root is there because it is allowed to remain.

Hebrews 12:15 reminds us, "See to it that no one falls short of the grace of God, and that no bitter root grows up to cause trouble and defile many."

How do we get a root of bitterness or unforgiveness in our spiritual drain field, and what does this look like on the outside? It may start with a legitimate hurt or wounding. It could be a parent or a caretaker, a friend or a trusted person, or a church member or church worker. It may be something that happened to us before we had the reasoning ability to process the hurt or offense. At some point, we are all hurt or offended or wounded. Some of us may be wounded as a child. We may or may not recognize it at the time. Later when we have the ability to think abstractly and to reason more complexly, we have the choice to process the hurt and forgive or to file it away in our memory bank. It may serve as a reminder of self-protection or self-reliance. Our wound may stay in our memory as a reminder to act a certain way or to be wary of certain people or situations. We may consider it a learning tool for our future behavior. The important point is that if we do not make the conscience effort to forgive the offender, we let that root remain. Like roots and plants in the world around us, they do not stay the same size forever.

On the outside, this growing root of unforgiveness may take on different forms. Some reactions to hurt are glaring and obvious like drug abuse or strong rebellious behaviors. Other reactions may be more subtle and concealed like sarcasm or passive-aggressive behavior.

If we are offended by a parent, it may start with a growing attitude or slight opposition to whatever they deem important. When we no longer live in the same house, we may talk less or visit less frequently. The progression is a growing emotional gap as well as a physical one. If we are offended by the church or someone associated with it, the scene may look very similar, only the progression may happen quicker. Eventually, that pipe is clogged and we cut off communication all together or limit it to a few hours on Christmas or Thanksgiving.

The posturing we took with the last offense will now feed into another area. Like the spreading of a root in one drain field pipe, now that it is full, it seeks another area to consume. We become comfortable with the position of being offended and may feel it is our right to be. Perhaps, we decide that church attendance is not that important. "I wasn't getting anything out of it anyway. There are only a bunch of hypocrites there, and I don't want to be one of them."

Certainly there are plenty of people there that can offend us in one way or another. It is best just to stay home. Maybe we really don't believe everything they were selling anyway. This pipe is clogged. Our life is great now because we have ridded ourselves of messy, clogged up unproductive relationships and acquaintances. We will just shut off service to those areas. We can get along fine without them.

The seed spreads. Their spouse is offensive. That package we thought we were getting when we got married has changed. They look different. They act different. When they are mad and say mean things, it sounds just like someone else that offended me, and I thought I got rid of that relationship. We argue and fight more and more. That person at the gym or at work is far more interesting. We are sure that a fresh start will make things much better. Maybe this person we are married to isn't our soul mate. We can certainly find a more suitable, agreeable person to spend the rest of our life with. We are smarter now. We can find a new mate that doesn't argue as much and that likes the same things and thinks the same way. It is time to seal off that clogged up pipe and move forward. We are actually getting pretty good at this pruning process.

This is how unforgiveness starts out small or contained and in the end brings chaos and destruction. As Christians, we are to forgive. Forgiveness, true forgiveness, eliminates the weed, and it never grows from there.

Stunted Growth

Do you know anyone that spent a large number years abusing drugs or alcohol? A common characteristic of someone that has abused drugs for many years is that their emotional growth seems to be trapped in that period of their life when the abuse started. It seems that until they get clean, they do not grow emotionally. I think a similar thing happens when we let the root of unforgiveness grow.

I believe it thwarts our spiritual growth and maturity until we clean out the spiritual drain field. We are spiritually stuck. And if we let it go on for a long period of time, I think we go backward.

A pastor showed me an example of the Christian life using a glass of milk and some liquid chocolate mix. In the example, the glass of milk represents our life before Christ. When we trust our life to Christ and become a Christian, the Holy Spirit indwells us. This is represented by pouring some chocolate mix into the white milk. But until the chocolate mix is stirred, the milk for the most part looks just like it did before. Also, if the milk is jostled a little initially but is quickly allowed to settle, it soon looks exactly like it did before. I think bitterness and unforgiveness is what keeps us looking and acting just like we did before we chose Christ.

What drew you to Christianity? What is it about the Christian beliefs and principles that made you want to make that decision? The most foundational basis of Christianity is that we are all sinners and separated from God. It is the forgiveness of our sins—past, present, and future—through Christ that we are restored to a right relationship with our creator. We want the forgiveness of our sins and we desire a relationship with God. We are asked to forgive others and to be humble. How can we want grace, mercy and forgiveness for ourselves, but refuse to extend grace, mercy and forgiveness to others? When we do not forgive, we hinder our relationship with others and with God.

I did an internet search for a certain white supremacist Ku Klux Klan member. I won't give his name, but suffice it to say that he is popular among his followers. The interesting thing was that he calls himself a pastor. His website lists all of his beliefs. If you did not look at who the pastor was, the list may initially look much like that of any other Christian church. Does this seem odd? He says that the Bible is the inspired word of God. That Jesus lived a blameless life and was crucified as payment of our sins. He acknowledges that Jesus rose from the dead and through Him we have forgiveness of sins. But somewhere, he takes a critical turn. I guess my question is how does someone accept God's forgiveness but embrace hatred toward another? We can easily pick out the contradictions in this thinking, but are we any less inconsistent when we hate or don't forgive for reasons other than race? Is there a difference if you hate someone because of something they did rather than because of who they are?

Who Have You Not Forgiven?

On that fateful day in 2001, Dean asked me a simple question, "Who have you not forgiven?"

My quick answer was, "No one." I felt fairly confident that this question was not relevant to my current situation. And additionally, I did not equate forgiveness of someone else to the struggles of my marriage. I assured Dean that before our next meeting, I would set aside a day to fast and pray to consider his question about forgiveness. I was true to my word.

Many of us have heard the popular refrain, "be careful what you wish for, you just may get it." A companion to this quip may be, "be careful what you ask God to show you, He is likely to answer your request."

I had set aside a day to fast and to ask God if there was someone I needed to forgive. My prayer was fairly simple. I asked God if He would reveal to me any areas of unforgiveness and anyone I needed to forgive. At about 10:00 a.m. that day, God answered that prayer.

When the memory first came to mind, I was a little startled. At first I was not sure why I began thinking of an experience from my childhood. The scene was very familiar to me; I just had not thought about it for many years.

I began thinking about a series of events I experienced at the tender age of about three and a half or four years of age. My oldest brother was very sick. There was a very good chance that he would die. My mother stayed with my brother at the hospital and my father worked at his job. To care for my siblings and me, my parents elected to have us put in foster care. Staying with strangers was not the worst part; it was not knowing how long I would be there or why.

When months went by and no one called to check on me, I felt abandoned and alone. Many times I cried myself to sleep. The people I lived with were nice, but I didn't know them and they didn't know me. It was the fear of the unknown that made the time go by so slowly. Christmas came and went, and it was not a very merry one. In all, I was in foster care for about six or seven months.

One day, the phone rang and the lady of the house looked at me and said I was going home. My brother had made it through the surgery and recovered enough to go home. Before long the social worker showed up, put me in her car, and drove me to be reunited with my parents and siblings. It was over. Maybe my parents didn't think I was aware enough to be bothered by the whole ordeal. Maybe they thought if they didn't talk about it, everything would be all right. Neither was correct.

My parents may or may not have done anything wrong. As a parent myself, I now know how easy it is to screw up. It is very easy to not say the right thing or to not respond to your child the right way. My hurt and feelings of abandonment were more a product of my own perceptions than any intentional wrongdoing by someone else.

God reminded me that I needed to forgive my parents. Maybe I would have made the same decision if I were in their shoes. There are many things we do not know and information we do not have when we look back with a twenty-twenty vision. Regardless of why things happened the way, they did. I knew at that moment God was calling me out. Did I really want to know who I had not forgiven? What was going to be my response to His answer to my fast? This was a pivotal moment for me. I knew immediately I had to forgive. I told God how much it hurt. I told Him how I felt for so many years. Then I said I forgive them and asked Him if He would forgive me too.

Additionally, I spent some time thinking through the situation with a different perspective. I tried to think about where God was during that time. Although I was scared, confused, and lonely, God had protected me. My foster family was never mean or abusive. They didn't mistreat me in any way. I had sad feelings, but I was very safe in the home I was placed.

In Daniel Goleman's book, *Social Intelligence*, he says that our memories are reconstructions. Goleman contends that when we retrieve a memory, we actually rewrite it a bit. He says that we update the past with the lens of our present concerns and understanding.

Each time we retrieve a memory, Goleman says that we start where it was last modified.[5]

Lee Trevino is quoted as saying, "The older I get, the better I used to be." This may be a funny quip, but it is actually a bit accurate in describing how we remember.

It is important to recognize that when it comes to our memory of past events, especially painful or unpleasant ones, that a few things we *remember* may not be true. We may have unconsciously changed the events given our present environment, understanding, and reference point. Furthermore, our goal on a personal level should be healing and growth, not harboring resentment, unforgiveness, and hurt.

Forgiveness 101

A pastor friend of mine, Philip Griffin,[6] in speaking about marriage, says that we go through a cycle in our relationship. First, we have the honeymoon phase. We are infatuated, in love, or ecstatic with our spouse. Then we have conflict with disagreements or arguing. After this, he says, we either move on toward true relationship, or we end the relationship and move on to the honeymoon phase with someone new.

I believe we go through this same cycle in all of our relationships. We can see this same scenario playing out with our job or our children. In the same way, our parents or our spouse or our boss was pretty happy with us when the relationship was new.

Then there is conflict. We disappoint our parents or our spouse or our boss. Our spouse and our children disappoint us. That sweet, innocent child turns into a mouthy, disrespectful youth. Or that

---

5 Social Intelligence by Daniel Goleman, A Bantam Book, October 2006, published by Bantam Dell, A Division of Random House, Inc. New York, New York. Page 78. From the work of Karim Nader at McGill University, cited by Joseph LeDoux, presentation at the meeting of the Consortium for Research on Emotional Intelligence in Organizations, Cambridge, Mass., December 14, 2004.

6 Pastor Philip Griffin, The Family Church, 2022 SW 122nd Street, Gainesville, FL 32607

wonderful, loving spouse that walked down the aisle and pledged their life to you is now arguing with you and saying some not-so-loving things. We can quit the job and get another one. The kids will eventually grow up and move out. We can, for the most part, avoid our parents for long stretches of time. What about the marriage? Do you stay in a marriage that is unhappy, unfulfilled, and volatile? No, you get divorced because that person must not have been your soul mate. Then after you disrupt lives and inflict pain and hurt and cause maximum damage, you can return to the honeymoon stage with someone new until the conflict rises to another crescendo with your new spouse.

The clogged spiritual drain field, built up resentment and unforgiveness, keeps us from moving past the conflict stage in our relationships. We are spiritually dead like an old addict that can't mature past where they were when they first started using. We can't get past conflicts in our many different relationships because of past unforgiveness.

How do we get out of this cycle and move into a deep and loving relationship in all areas of our life? The answer is twofold. First, you have to come humbly to God. This is the first step in every situation. The best way to begin to fix a situation is to tell God that you can't fix it. We truly are powerless to do much of anything. The first step is to turn it over to God and submit fully to Him. Admit to God and to yourself that you screwed up and needed help. Come to God on your knees with nothing but a brokenness and a humble spirit. When you tell God that He is in control and not you, then He can do something. Joel 2:12–13 (NIV) says, "'Now therefore,' says the Lord, 'turn to me with all your heart, with fasting and weeping and mourning. So rend your heart and not your garments.'" And then in the same chapter, verse 25 (NKJV) says, "So I will restore to you the years that the swarming locusts hath eaten."

This is a common theme throughout the Bible. This is the main point of this book. If we turn to God, with sincerity of heart, and come to Him humbly and broken, He will restore. God can restore what the locusts have eaten. He can make things better than they were before.

The second step is to forgive. God forgave us more than we could ever forgive someone else. Start with your earliest memory and consider who you may have unforgiveness toward. This may be a parent or a caretaker. This may be a sibling or a friend. For some, it may be a particular group or a race of people. There are races of people in history that have had terrible things done to them. Today in many parts of our world, people are tortured and killed because of their religion or the color of their skin.

The choice we have is to forgive or not to forgive. When we choose not to forgive, we are setting ourselves up as judge, jury, and executioner. We claim that we have all of the facts and evidence and that we are the best to administer justice. We are taking God's place in the matter. Is it any wonder why our relationship with God is affected as a result?

When we choose to forgive, we relinquish the outcome and the punishment and the circumstances to God and His control. We do not condone bad behavior or excuse it; we just let God take care of it as He sees fit. What we can do is trust that God's way of justice and judgement is superior to ours. He knows many things that we do not. We can choose to trust God and not elevate our self. In the larger view, the issue really isn't about the other person anyway. It is a question of my trust in God. Do I trust God to be in control? Do I trust that God knows what is going on? Do I trust that God loves me?

We have to forgive. We can't just forgive some people or most people; we must forgive everyone and anyone who has every offended us in any way. If you are holding something back, it is the same as holding it all back. Do not just forgive those that in your mind *deserves* it. Forgive everyone. This takes faith. When we forgive, among other things, we are saying that we trust God to take care of the situation. We are trusting God to heal the hurt and to take care of us. We are trusting God to deal with the offender in His way and we trust that His way is the right way.

The freedom comes in that we are not mentally shackled to the situation. We are no longer tormented by the angst or ill feelings toward another. The desire for repayment is not constantly stifling the joy in our heart. This is the freedom that true forgiveness brings.

Servant of the King

In Mathew 18, Peter asks Jesus how many times he should forgive. The answer that Jesus gives is seventy times seven. Then Jesus tells the story of a king who wanted to settle his accounts. The king had a servant that owed him ten thousand bags of gold. Since the servant could not pay what he owed, it was ordered that the servant and his wife and children be sold as payment. The servant begs for patience, and the king dismisses the debt completely and allows him to go free. Then the servant goes out and finds someone that owes him a fraction of what he owed the king. When the person that owed him money couldn't pay it, the man had him thrown in prison.

Of course, this gets back to the king, and the king says, "You wicked servant. I cancelled all that debt of yours because you begged me. Shouldn't you have had mercy on your fellow servant just as I had with you?"

The king then turns the man over to be tortured until he can repay the debt. The amount of debt we owed can never be repaid. Then in Mathew 18: 35, Jesus says, "This is how my heavenly father will treat each of you unless you forgive your brother or sister from your heart." That little prepositional phrase at the end of the sentence means not just in words but to truly mean it. Only through the Holy Spirit can we truly forgive others. We are human. Sometimes others do things that really hurt us. It is impossible to forgive on our own.

Joseph

In the last few chapters of Genesis, we read the story of Joseph. Joseph is sold into slavery by his brothers who then tell their father that he was killed by a wild animal. They are jealous of him and his self-elevating dreams. Joseph becomes a servant in the household of Potiphar, an officer of Pharaoh in Egypt. When Joseph refuses the advances of Potiphar's wife, he is wrongly accused and thrown into prison. In prison, he interprets dreams for Pharaoh's baker and cupbearer that are in prison with him. He tells the cupbearer that in three days, he will be set free and return to the Pharaoh's service. And he tells the baker that his dream means that in three days, he will be relieved of his head, impaled on a stake and fed to the birds of the air.

Both interpretations come to pass, but the cupbearer forgets about Joseph. Two years later, Pharaoh had a dream that no one can tell him the meaning of. It is then that the cupbearer remembers Joseph. Joseph tells the king the meaning of his strange dreams. He tells Pharaoh that there will be seven years of plenty followed by seven years of drought. The king then puts Joseph second in command in all of Egypt.

Years later when the famine is severe, Joseph's brothers come to Egypt to buy grain. They have to ask him if they can buy grain, but they do not recognize him as their brother. He tests them to see their hearts. When Joseph reveals himself to his brothers, they are afraid. But Joseph makes it clear to them that he has already forgiven them. He tells them that what they meant for evil, God used for good. He came to Egypt to help preserve their family.

This is an example of what forgiveness looks like. Joseph is taken away from his family and sent to a foreign land as a slave. He is falsely accused and put in prison. When he has the upper hand against the very brothers that sent him away, he chooses forgiveness.

Renee Napier Modern Examples

An internet search for "story behind Mathew West's song, Forgiveness"[7] will produce the story of Renee Napier. One of her twin teen daughters was killed by a drunk driver. First was Renee and then the rest of her family sought out the offender in prison to express their forgiveness toward him. The story doesn't end with seemingly heartfelt words of "I forgive you." It was then backed up with Renee working on his behalf to get his sentence reduced. True

---

[7] www.onlinechristiansongs.com/2013/03/story-behind-song-forgiveness-matthew.html

forgiveness means that the debt was paid. If the debt is paid, we are not still looking for compensation. In this story, Renee was then free to show love and compassion to the offender. Her actions demonstrate total forgiveness. Sometimes, forgiveness gives way to compassion. When we look past the offence, we may see the hurt and unforgiveness that the offender experienced which then led to their actions toward someone else. This can only come from the spirit of God working deep in a person's heart.

In recent headlines, a gunman killed nine people at a Bible study at the Emanuel African Methodist Episcopal Church in Charleston, South Carolina. One of those who were killed was a small child. It is hard to imagine the hurt and heartache for those that had family members or friends killed in such a tragic way. Two things about this story stood out to me. First, through the pain and tears, many of those that were affected by the actions of the gunman expressed words of forgiveness toward him. Second, buried in the story was a few sentences about the shooter's broken family and the hurt and anger about his parents' divorce. They are an example to the world of what forgiveness toward someone who meant you harm looks like. They are an example of what Jesus asks of us.

The examples of Louis Zamperini, the Amish at Nickel Mines, Renee Napier and her teenage daughter, and the African American church in South Carolina are all models of people that get it. They all understand that we have to forgive and that forgiveness of others is what sets us free.

Quite honestly, for many of us, these stories pale in comparison to who we need to forgive or for what. The ultimate description of forgiveness is God's forgiveness of us through Jesus. The bottom line is that if we want to be forgiven, we must forgive others. When we do, we are set free.

Have I Really Forgiven Them?

You will know when you have truly and completely forgiven someone. There is nothing blocking your relationship with them and any memory of the situation does not bring hurt or pain. If you cannot remember without hurt or pain and there is a barrier to the relationship, forgiveness has not taken place in your heart. True forgiveness usually produces compassion toward the other person. Forgiveness is faith in action. It is trusting God and not relying on ourselves for comfort or justice or peace or redemption. It is saying to God, "You are in control, and You know best."

As Christians, we are called to forgive. We cannot accept God's forgiveness of all of our sins—past, present, and future—and then say we are unwilling to forgive someone else. We cannot say we want forgiveness but then embrace hatred toward someone else.

We know what unforgiveness looks like as well. We only have to look at the world around us. We see unforgiveness in broken families and in crime and destruction on the nightly news. Our prisons are full of stories of unforgiveness. But sometimes, unforgiveness lays seemingly quiet and dormant in the recesses of our heart. It may go unnoticed for a time. The only evidence of its existence is an outburst here and there or a bad attitude. But unforgiveness blocks our relationship with God. We can go through the motions of being a Christian and having a relationship with God, but it is empty. Without forgiveness, there is a waning in our desire to seek God. The wanting to daily seek and know God is a chore and not a joy. Until the day when the festering seed of unforgiveness is a giant weed, the size of a tree cannot be ignored. Then the destruction that the locusts have caused is evident for all to see.

We have all heard stories of someone that seemingly had everything going right in their lives until they don't. A seemingly happy couple files for divorce, a respected person in the church runs off with another woman. Whatever the surprise event is, we all have seen it. When I was a teen, my church group leader left his wife and three small kids one day and never returned. Everyone is the audience to the explosion. They just didn't recognize the slow clogging of the spiritual drain field that started years before.

How do we get to right relationship with God and people in our lives? Set aside time for sincere prayer and seeking. I suggest a time of fasting. Start with your earliest memory and work forward. Ask God to bring to mind anyone who you need to forgive. Sometimes we need to forgive ourselves. Some like Charlie Roberts may be mad at God. Ask yourself, "What do I complain about the most?" Ask yourself where in your life there are broken relationships. What memories bring forth pain or hurt feelings? The answer to these questions will reveal who you have not forgiven and where work needs to be done.

When we have forgiveness in our hearts, it opens up our relationship to God. The milk is stirred up and there is a visible difference that others can see. Where you previously became quickly offended or angry, now it doesn't seem to matter as much or to be of much importance.

Secondly, it changes your relationship with others. When the resentment is gone and the hurt is gone, it changes everything. This is the secret. This is how you move past the conflict stage in an area of your life to the true relationship phase. As a result, the relationship gets better and better. What you will notice is that the conflicts are fewer and fewer and less and less severe. You will then notice the relationship getting deeper and deeper. When you forgive, it is you that is set free.

I will tell you another secret. When you forgive, it shows on your face and in your actions. When you have been through the process of getting rid of worthless baggage and you live a life of forgiveness toward others, it shows. The other side of that is that when you have fully forgiven, you know what unforgiveness looks like. You can spot it from across the room. Like an ex-addict can spot a user in a second, a person that is truly free from the bondage of unforgiveness can spot the poison in others quickly. That is when you can help someone else through the same process.

David, at the end of Psalms 139, asks God to search him and know his heart. To clean out our spiritual drain field of hidden, bitter root, and unforgiveness, we have to ask God to search our heart. In Joel 2, the message is to rend (tear) your heart, not your garments. God wants the work to be done on the inside, not a show on the outside. Then God promises to restore what the locusts have eaten. He will restore what has been destroyed by our wrongdoing.

I strongly suggest this process be done with a trusted, close fellow Christian. This can be done alone, but it is much more effective as a pair or a trio. It goes without saying that men work with men and women with women.

First, we have to identify where the problem is. Search your heart through prayer and fasting. If we ask God to show us where we have been hurt or offended and who we hold something against, He will answer that prayer.

After you have identified specific areas in your life where you have been hurt or wounded, take time to hurt or grieve the wound that caused the offense in the first place. You have acknowledged that you were hurt. Now through the power of the Holy Spirit, tell God that you forgive those that offended or hurt you. Tell God what they did, how it hurt you, and tell Him you forgive. If you experienced a hurtful or terrible event in your life that caused you hurt and pain, look for where God was in that situation. Identify where God protected you or was with you and thank Him for it.

Many times, those that are trying to help someone through this process want to identify the hurt and move on to forgiveness. I think it is important to take the time necessary to feel that hurt and acknowledge it. When someone has been abused or abandoned or neglected or whatever the offense was, it hurts. It is important to work through the hurt as well as the forgiveness.

Second, the one thing that cleans out our spiritual drain field and makes it shinny and new is forgiveness. It is paramount that you fully and completely forgive those that have wronged you. The Bible has plenty to say about forgiveness. Mathew 5:22 says, "But I tell you that anyone who is angry with a brother or sister will be subject to judgement." Mathew 5:23–24 says, "Therefore, if you are offering your gift at the altar and there remember that your brother or sister has something against you, leave your gift there in front of the altar. First go and be reconciled to them; then come and offer your gift."

In Luke 11, Jesus is teaching the disciples to pray. In verse 4, he says, "Forgive us our sins for we also forgive everyone who sins against us."

When Jesus taught His disciples to pray, in addition to acknowledging God as who He is and asking for God's provisions, Jesus also says we ask for forgiveness for ourselves as we also forgive others. It all goes together. We cannot acknowledge God, thank Him for His blessings, ask for His daily provisions, ask to be forgiven and leave it at that. It is like a combination lock that you got all of the numbers lined up but one. If you do not forgive others, your prayers are not unlocked. Mathew 6:14–15 (NIV) puts it pretty clearly. "For if you forgive other people when they sin against you, your heavenly Father will also forgive you. But if you do not forgive others their sins, your Father will not forgive your sins."

We can try to make those verses mean something else or quantify the word *sin* or the word *forgive*. I must admit, I was a Christian for many years before I truly embraced these verses. But if we are Christian (like Christ), we are called to forgive. As Jesus hung on the cross, He did not need to be forgiven, but He still prayed for the forgiveness of those who put Him there. We are to emulate Christ.

I think we sometimes have a habit of pointing out the bad in a situation without acknowledging the good. This is especially true if we are considering someone we are not fond of. If we recall a poor childhood memory or event that is the source of much pain, there may have been God's protection or God's provision for us in that time that we have not recognized. If we really reflect on the events of our lives where we felt hurt or alone or when something happened that caused pain in one way or another, we can usually see where God was really there with us in that situation.

Let me bring this back to the marriage. I believe that when there is trouble in a relationship like a marriage, it is not an isolated incident. That is why I focus on other areas of unforgiveness and start with the earliest. I think that typically, we have a pattern of unforgiveness and choosing offense, and that when it shows up in a marriage, it is just the next clog in the drain field. When all relationships are clear of offense and we have an attitude of forgiveness and love toward all others, it naturally heals the marriage as well. When our heart is right, we are honoring our commitment to the covenant. When our heart isn't right, only the circumstances and the characters change but the problem does not.

Sometimes, people say, "Yes, but my spouse is far from God and headed in the other direction." Marriage is not fifty-fifty. You need to work on it 100 percent. Do not worry about the other person. Ask for forgiveness from your spouse without expecting a reciprocal request. If your spouse ask for forgiveness, of course, grant it. But don't make your forgiveness contingent on them asking for it. Your part is to forgive everyone as God has forgiven you. When you have truly forgiven all others, then God can hear your prayers and restore what the locusts have eaten.

When God restores, He restores in a big way. He makes things better than before. He blesses more than before.

Many times, the person who hurt or offended me is acting the way they are because they were hurt or offended and did not forgive. If I do not forgive, it hurts me and continues the cycle. In the end, if I do not forgive, I will have to ask someone else for forgiveness for the very same thing. How many people do you know that are mad at their parents for getting a divorce and they themselves get divorced later in life?

Forgiveness will set you free and give you the solid foundation that you must have to have a healthy marriage and a growing and maturing life. You cannot have peace on the surface without peace in your innermost being.

When you understand and embrace forgiveness, it will transform your mind, your actions, and your life.

Questions for Discussion

1. Describe some of the happiest memories of your childhood—how you felt and why.
2. Describe some of the unhappiest memories from your childhood—how you felt and why.
3. Discuss a person or persons from your youth that offended you and why.
4. Are you often called callous, critical, or sarcastic? If so, where do you think it stems from?
5. Discuss a time where you were hurt, offended, or faced difficulties and where you think God may have been in that situation.
6. Who do you need to forgive?

CHAPTER 6

LASTING CHANGE

> But seek first his kingdom and his righteousness and all these things will be given to you as well. Therefore, do not worry about tomorrow, for tomorrow will worry about itself. Each day has enough trouble of its own.
> —Matthew 6:33–34

The last chapter was about forgiveness. We saw many examples of people who chose to forgive others in some extremely tough circumstances. It is not an easy choice in that it involves pain and hurt and feelings. However, the choice to forgive is ultimately the only choice.

When we come to Christ, we are aware of our hopeless condition and we ask God to forgive us and accept us as clean through Jesus's shed blood. This begins a new and wonderful relationship with God, Jesus, and the Holy Spirit. As a result, we are a changed person with a heart for the things of God. We have a desire for loving God and growing in that relationship.

Then we hold back forgiveness on someone who has wronged us. We focus on the hurt or the perceived injustice, and we become the judge. Moving forward, this blocks our relationship with God. We may still attend church or sing in the choir or hold some position of authority within the church, but the relationship and the closeness is not there as it was in the beginning. At this point, we are faking it. We are operating on our own power. We can imitate words and actions we've picked up over the years, and no one will know that our heart is truly far from God. How will someone sitting next to me in the church pew know that I haven't opened my Bible to read it in six months?

Soon, our power is not enough. Before long, we know the truth and it bothers us. We question why we feel the way we do. We wonder why we do not have the joy we once had. Why did I once want to do whatever I could in service to God, and now I'd rather sleep in on Sunday morning?

And then you take an inventory of the other aspects of your life. The closest person to you is your spouse. It is hard to hide your true self from the person that is there when you wake up and when you go to sleep. You spend so much time with this person—things are going to come up. They know where your vulnerabilities are. They know almost everything about you. At this point, you wonder why I do not have the joy I once had with my spouse. Why did I once want to do whatever I could for the love of my life, and now I regret being tied together with them?

Do you see a pattern? You may think the two things are not related, but I assure you they are. A similar pattern will play itself out in all of your relationships—parents, friends, work, etc.

This is how we go from energetic Christian, wonderful husband/wife, great friend, and stable person to divorced, broken relationships, and no interest in God or church. We made the wrong decision when we were wronged or hurt by someone else. That is the point at which we let the unforgiveness root to begin growing in our spiritual drain field.

At first, our decision not to forgive someone was a personal decision and others may not have been aware of it. My initial decision of not forgiving someone is not visible to others in any tangible way. But after that decision has taken root in my life and grown and matured the way roots do, it is obvious for all to see. Now people that barely know me can see the effects of unforgiveness in my life. They may call it dysfunction or divorce or by some other name, but it is the same root.

Isn't it amazing? An event or a cross word or hurtful action by one person can set a course that plays itself out years, maybe decades later, as destruction and dysfunction and into lives that were never part of the original occurrence.

At this point, we tell ourselves that the problem cannot be repaired. Maybe we think too much damage has been done. We believe we will be better off starting over. We change jobs, we change churches or stop going to church all together, and we get a divorce and a new spouse. We solve the problems in our life with our superior worldly wisdom. Lives are disrupted, damaged, or worse. We try to jettison ourselves from the situation and pretend that time will heal all wounds. Did time miraculously turn the unforgiveness root into a beautiful fruit tree? We hope that we can just forget the whole mess, and it will somehow go away.

This is clearly not the right answer. The better choice is the harder choice. But in the end, it is the one that brings about a superior result. Go back to the first offense. Some of us immediately know where that point is. Some of us have buried it so deep and covered it so well. We need to spend time discovering when we first chose to not forgive a wrongdoing. If you humbly pray and seek God, He will reveal what that point in your life was.

As you return to the point of unforgiveness, this time make a different choice. Choose to forgive. Sometimes we can tell the other person that we forgive them. Many times that may not be possible to tell someone directly for one reason or another. Either way, we can tell God that we do. In turn, it is then us that must ask for forgiveness. Forgiveness from God for holding on to that offense for so long and forgiveness from others we have hurt as a result.

And going forward, we quickly forgive when life happens, and we are at that point again. No matter how big or how small the offense is, we choose to forgive. We make the choice to live as the Bible instructs us to love others as Christ loves us. We make the choice to forgive others as we have been forgiven. We choose right over wrong, love over indifference, life over death, and God's ways over our own. Sometimes forgiving can seem hard to do. There are many of us that may struggle to forgive, especially when the hurt is traumatic, extremely hurtful, or new.

I sometimes get the question, "How do I forgive?"

I refer to the eighteenth chapter of Matthew, where Jesus compares unforgiveness to the unmerciful servant. We owed more than we could ever pay. My own sin and need for forgiveness surpasses anything I feel I am owed by another. If we reflect on the words of Christ in this chapter, we understand there is no comparison of our transgressions toward God and someone else's offenses toward us.

Additionally, I am not called to be the judge. God is the only one true righteous judge. For me, to take on that role is to elevate myself to a dangerous position. It is a reflection of my lack of faith and trust. When I make myself the judge, I am exhibiting pride and not humility. When I hold on to an offense, it is at the core, a heart issue. It is not truly about the other person; it is about me.

I can respond to an offense by another by being an example of Jesus and offer forgiveness; or I can harden my heart, put myself on the throne, and hinder my own relationship with God.

There are past hurts that we need to forgive and newer, more recent offenses to address. Whether old wounds or new ones, the process is the same.

The benefit of a past offense is the passage of time can sometimes give us better insight and clarity of God's presence in the situation. Many times, when we are in the midst of a circumstance, we do not see the workings of God as clearly. Many years later, we may be more aware of God's hand during that time.

A general road map for working through forgiveness is to first acknowledge the hurt. Many times, we need to start with just telling God how we feel. Depending on the circumstance, we may need to grieve the hurt. Then we ask God to forgive us for holding on to it and to help us to forgive the other person. Next is to ask God to show you where he was in that situation, or if it is current, ask him to be present in it. Finally, ask God to work in that person's life. If a hurt is deep, it may be necessary to revisit the process a number of times.

The point is to have a right heart toward God. God gives grace to the humble. He lifts up the brokenhearted, not so with the prideful. A prideful heart resist God. Go back to Joel 2:12–13. Our part is to humble ourselves.

God can restore the destruction. He can restore what sin has destroyed. To do this, we have to have our heart aligned with Him. We cannot harbor unforgiveness in any fashion. There is no need to. We have been forgiven more than can be counted.

Here is the point I want to make. The person that you married, you loved them more than anyone else. But so many times, we let the root of unforgiveness grow in our spiritual drain field. We start by rejecting someone in our past and not forgiving them. We still love our spouse and many other of the channels of relationships are unaffected. But as we get more comfortable with the posture of deciding who deserves forgiveness and who does not, two things happen. First, our relationship with God is blocked and the Holy Spirit is silent within us. Second, other relationships begin to slowly suffer the same fate as the first one. The bitter root of unforgiveness that we are cultivating begins to grow in new areas.

Before long, our family and friends become distant and the relationships are broken. And at some point, that spouse that you once loved more than anything else is now an enemy.

The answer is simple, but it is also many times very difficult. Accept God's forgiveness and freely extend the same forgiveness to others. God is the ultimate judge. He will decide what the punishment should be. Leave it up to Him. He can take care of things so much better than we can.

Unforgiveness will change your life. It will take a couple that loves each other, thinks about each other, and can't stand to be apart and change them into a fighting and hurtful pair that want nothing to do with each other. Unforgiveness will change a life of love to a life of distain or hate.

Forgiveness can change lives and hearts and futures. Forgiveness can heal and join hearts and change a couple to a deeper love and an unimaginable deeper relationship. Forgiveness can break a pattern of dysfunction and change generations going forward.

There was a time when my wife and I almost got divorced. We were one day away from signing the final papers in front of a judge.

I have been asked how exactly we transitioned from ready to divorce to a relationship of loving and caring and being best friends.

The short answer is that I first had to come to a point of surrender. I had reached a low point and quite literally cried out to God. I came to Him humbly and acknowledged my way wasn't working. I agreed that I would do whatever God asked of me no matter what. I purposed in my heart to put God first and trust in Him and to not worry about what the circumstances looked like. At the time, the circumstances looked hopeless.

The very next thing I did was to begin as far back as I could remember and forgive anyone I felt had wronged me in any way. As each person or situation came to mind, I thought it out and told God that I fully forgive that person and then I prayed for them. I asked God to forgive me for holding on to a hurt for so long.

An important point to make here is that the only person I had control over was myself. The only person's mind-set I could change was my own. Furthermore, the only person I needed to focus on was myself and my relationship with God. I did not need to clutter my mind or be concerned with what someone else may need to do or not do. I did not even need to be concerned with how anyone else may receive my change of heart.

That is when our marriage was restored. Yes, it did take some time to work back to a cohesive and trusting relationship, but the tide had changed, and we were on the road back to where we needed to be. There was still much work, but every day was easier and better than the one before.

I wrote this book to tell others the secret to a wonderful marriage and a contented heart.

When you forgive, God can change your life. When you come to God with a humble and contrite heart, He can grow you, use you, and bless you. Then God can restore what the locusts have eaten. He can restore the damage that has been done and make all things new.

Questions for Discussion

1. Am I truly focused solely on my condition before God, or am I also concerned with where someone else may be lacking in growth?
2. Have I taken a complete inventory of my life and fully forgiven anyone and everyone that may have wronged me in any way starting with my earliest recollection?
3. Am I the best husband, wife, son, daughter, or friend that I can be to others?
4. Do I have an accountability partner that can speak truth and love into my life where I need it most?
5. How can others pray for me?

CONCLUSION

Mental health professionals tell us that to have a sense of well-being we need someone to love, something to do, and something to look forward to. When one or more of these things is missing in our lives, it creates dissatisfaction and unhappiness in our lives.

We fulfill these needs by marrying the person that we love, and we expect them to love us back. We find something to do in our occupation or in volunteer work or something meaningful to fill our days. Additionally, we look forward to promotions or more money to spend on more stuff. Sometimes we look forward to different milestones like our kid's graduation or our retirement.

Certainly if these innate desires are universally within all of us, they were put there by our creator. However, when we are not in a right relationship with God, they are perverted and distorted. God wants us to love Him above all else. We need to have jobs to pay bills and exist, but our primary mission is to do God's work here on earth. And ultimately, we are looking forward to heaven and an eternity with Him.

When we are not in a right relationship with God, we look to others for love or we look for increased satisfaction from our jobs or careers. We look forward to bigger and bigger earthly rewards and comforts. This leaves us feeling empty, and we continue to seek an answer.

Typically, we strive for control, comfort, or importance in our worldly pursuits. These are our modern-day idols. We seek them to the exclusion of other things. An idol is something that takes the place of God. When we put ourselves in the place of God, we are the idol. We become lovers of self. A good method for self-identifying possible idols is to answer the following question: What is the thing or things that I have that I would be devastated if it or they were taken away from me?

When we get married, we are happy, confident, and the future is full of promise. We make vows to each other to be there through thick and thin, richer or poorer, sickness and in health. Maybe we should say, "I promise to stay with you when you gain weight or lose your hair. I promise to stay by your side when you act like a jerk or call me unpleasant names. I promise to love you when I really don't like you." We do not think of such unpleasantries on a day full of love and happy thoughts. On the contrary, most of us think that will never happen to us.

I think most of us that walk down the aisle and make those commitments are not truly thinking of the covenant relationship we are entering to. We do not fully understand that what we are saying is, "I will be with you, no matter what." "I am truly going to be your partner until the day I die."

We have a mind-set that says, "As long as my needs are met and I am happy, I will be here for my spouse." The truth is that a day will come when your needs are not met. A day will come when you will be disappointed and the other person will let you down. The self-centered mentality says, "They aren't who I thought they were, and I am not getting what I want, so it is time to go back to taking care of number one."

At the core of every divorce is a heart problem. If we have love and forgiveness in our hearts, we would not get divorced. It starts with unforgiveness getting a foothold in our hearts. The Bible says, "In your anger do not sin. Do not let the sun go down while you are still angry. And do not give the devil a foothold" (Eph. 4:26–27). I think the "foothold" is something that we allowed many years before we even knew the person we are married to. It is the anger from an offense that gives evil the room to grow in our hearts. To fix the present, we must get rid of the "foothold" from the past.

In summary, I believe there are three things that are at the very core of divorce. If we get these three things right, we have a good shot at having a wonderfully successful marriage and partnership.

First and foremost, we must look to God to fill that God-sized hole in our life. If we expect our partner to fill a need that only a relationship with God can fill, it is not going to have the desired outcome. A good job or things or money will not fill that void either. Understanding this and putting things in their proper order is the first step in any healthy relationship.

The second principle is that a marriage is a covenant, an unbreakable promise between the couple and God. It is not a promise based on performance or one person's benefit. It is not based on what you do or do not receive. It is an unbreakable promise that you will be there as a support and partner come what may.

And finally, the key to all successful relationships is to have an attitude of forgiveness always and toward everyone. Clean up any clogged up spiritual drain fields from your past and go forward with a forgiving attitude. Understand that we owe more than we could ever repay, and we need to be gracious and forgiving to those that offend us.

This is the building blocks for a healthy marriage. It is not fifty-fifty. Fifty-fifty says, "I am going this far, and you have to meet me in the middle." Marriage is you giving 100 percent. If you do these things and give 100 percent to your marriage in everything you do, God will restore what the locusts have eaten. Do not worry about what the other half is doing or not doing. Pray for your spouse and let God take care of it.

Linda Waite of the University of Chicago conducted a study of unhappy marriages.[8] She tested the hypothesis that someone in an unhappy marriage had two choices to consider: staying married and miserable or divorced and happier. The study found no evidence that people who divorced were any happier than those that did not. Furthermore, she found evidence that two-thirds of those that considered their marriage unhappy but remained married reported their marriage happier just five years later.

---

[8] The Case for Marriage, Linda J. Waite and Maggie Gallagher, published by Doubleday a division of Random House, Inc. 2000. Page 148.

The Bible says, "Not everyone who says to me, 'Lord, Lord,' will enter the kingdom of heaven. But only the one who does the will of my Father who is in heaven" (Matt. 7:21–22, NIV). To do the will of the Father, we must first know Him and have a relationship with Him. The Bible says we are to forgive as we have been forgiven. It then says that if we do not forgive, God will not forgive us. Unforgiveness in any form is not the will of the Father. Divorce and the anger, resentment and destruction that goes with it is not the will of the Father. If you cannot forgive, then it is important to examine the basis of your relationship with God. When you do forgive everyone completely, the result is freedom that is unexplainable. The result of forgiveness is love.

God wants us to love Him with all of our heart, soul, and mind. When we focus on the right thing, God can restore what the locusts have eaten.

I want to end with a couple tips for after you have done all of this. I have a few suggestions based on where you are and what needs to be done. The first step is fully understanding and embracing forgiveness. It is important to have an attitude of forgiveness so that no weeds will spring up. I like the quote by Andrew Bonar that says, "Be as watchful after the war as before the battle." Guard your heart that you do not let an offense creep back in. One of the best resources for identifying areas of hurt and offense and working through them in forgiveness is the Cleansing Stream program that is offered by different churches. Try to find somewhere in your area that offers the Cleansing Stream program. If you attend it, make sure you set aside time to attend the retreat at the end. It is the most vital part of the whole package. Taking the classes and not going to the retreat is like studying a course and not getting the hands on experience of an internship.

Next, if you are looking for better ways to understand your spouse and how to relate in a way that best speaks to him or her, pick up a copy of Gary Chapman's book, *The Five Love Languages*. This book will help you identify what speaks love to your spouse. Let's say my wife feels love when I spend quality time with her. But I don't take much time out of my schedule to spend with her. Instead, I buy her things that I think will make her happy. If I am not speaking to what helps her feel love, I am not doing much good.

I started this book by promising a direction for fixing a failing or unhappy marriage. I know that if you do all of these things without skipping any steps or taking a shortcut, the change will be phenomenal. And if you are the only one out of a two-person marriage that wants to fix it, do not be deterred. If that is the case, then you do 100 percent of the work. Do everything step by step without being distracted by lack of participation from the other spouse. Do not get divorced. Forgive fully, love without reservation, and seek God with all your heart.

Thank you. Now share it.

ABOUT THE AUTHOR

Mark Ulmer grew up in Tennessee and Florida. He graduated from the University of Central Florida in Orlando in 1997 with a degree in business and a major in finance. He has been married to his wife, Karen, for more than thirty years, and they have one son who lives in Redmond, Washington, with his wife.

He lives in Gainesville, Florida, where he works as a realtor and leads a Friday morning Bible study for men.

Mark has a passion for sharing his message of forgiveness, restoration, and relationship through group talks and one-on-one mentorship with other men.

He was inspired to write this book after his near-divorce experience and learning from his own struggles with unforgiveness, anger, and resentment. He wants to share with others how they can move from a fractured and divisive marriage to one of love and unity that models the love of Christ to others.

CPSIA information can be obtained
at www.ICGtesting.com
Printed in the USA
JSHW021221140822
29215JS00002B/116